# THERAPY DOGS

## Training Your Dog to Help Others
## 2nd Edition

## Kathy Diamond Davis

Dogwise Publishing
Wenatchee, Washington U.S.A.
www.dogwise.com

Dogwise™
Publishing

**Therapy Dogs**
**Training Your Dog to Reach Others, 2ⁿᵈ Edition**
Kathy Diamond Davis

**Dogwise Publishing**
A Division of Direct Book Service, Inc.
PO Box 2778
701B Poplar
Wenatchee, Washington 98807
509-663-9115
Website: http://www.dogwisepublishing.com
Email: info@dogwisepublishing.com

Indexing by Elaine Melnick "The Index Lady"

© 2002, Kathy Diamond Davis

Library of Congress Cataloging-in-Publication Data

Davis, Kathy Diamond.
Therapy dogs: training your dog to reach others / by Kathy Diamond
Davis.— 2nd ed.
    p. cm.
Includes bibliographical references and index.
    ISBN 1-929242-05-0
1. Dogs—Therapeutic use. 2. Dogs—Training. I. Title.
    RM931.D63 D38 2002

                                        2002004740


Printed in Canada

# Table of Contents

## Introduction

AN UPDATE ................................................................ 3

    Therapy Dogs: A Definition ............................................. 3

    A Disclaimer And A Note On Style ................................... 5

## Chapter 1

BENEFITS THERAPY DOGS PROVIDE ........................... 7

    Orientation To Reality ..................................................... 7

    Focal Point For Attention-deficit Problems ..................... 8

    Morale ........................................................................... 9

    Antidote To Depression ................................................. 9

    Cooperation ................................................................ 10

    Social Stimulation ....................................................... 10

    Need For Touch .......................................................... 14

    Socialize Children To Dogs .......................................... 15

    Working With Therapists .............................................. 16

    Incentive ..................................................................... 17

    Getting Out Of Yourself ............................................... 17

    Practicing Physical Skills ............................................. 19

    Happy Anticipation ...................................................... 20

    Emotional Support To Staff And Family ........................ 21

## Chapter 2

WHAT KIND OF DOG? ................................................ 23

    Breeds Suited For Therapy Work .................................. 23

    Choosing A Puppy For Therapy Dog Work ................... 26

    Sources For Young Adult Dogs .................................... 28

    Trainability .................................................................. 29

    Somebody's Baby ........................................................ 30

    Benefits To The Dog ................................................... 31

    Benefits To The Handler .............................................. 31

    Competition Vs. Therapy Dog ...................................... 33

    Benefits To The Community ......................................... 36

    What If You Don't Have A Dog ..................................... 37

Publicity ........................................................ 38
The Indoor Dog ............................................. 39
Parasite Control ............................................ 40
The Veterinarian ........................................... 41
Is Therapy Dog Work For You? ..................... 44

# Chapter 3

VISITS AS A GROUP ........................................... 47
The Right Facility For You And Your Dog ...... 47
Disaster Work ................................................ 50
Join An Established Group ............................ 51
Dealing With Other Dogs ............................... 53
Standards And Uninterrupted Service ........... 55
Insurance ...................................................... 56
Working With Facility Staff ............................ 57
Indoor Or Outdoor Visits? ............................ 59
Education, Entertainment Or Therapy? ......... 60
Cooperation Among Groups .......................... 60
Does This Group Make You Proud? .............. 61

# Chapter 4

VISITS WITH ONE DOG ...................................... 63
Win Approval Of A Group .............................. 64
Working With The Staff .................................. 65
Quieter, Less Disruption To Facility Routine ... 66
Stronger Focus ............................................. 67
Limits ............................................................ 67
Rooms Versus Meeting Areas ...................... 68
Making Changes ........................................... 70
The Approach ............................................... 71
Working With Children ................................... 73
First Visits Awkward ..................................... 75
Facility Choices ............................................ 75
The Leash ..................................................... 76

# Chapter 5

CONDITIONING THE DOG TO HANDLING ...... 79
Motivators: Food, Praise, Petting, And Play ... 79
Teaching The Dog To Remain Still ............... 83
Picking Up The Dog ...................................... 85
Games To Play... Work That Tail! ................. 88
Attention, Release ........................................ 90

Retrieving ...................................................... 92
Safety Hints For Retrieving During Visits ...................... 97
To Tug Or Not To Tug? .......................................... 98
Inhibiting The Bite ............................................ 100
Teasing As A Form Of Play ...................................... 104
All Kinds Of Sights, Scents And Sounds ......................... 105
Correction ..................................................... 108
A Cuddle A Day ................................................. 112

# Chapter 6

BASIC CONTROL FOR THERAPY WORK ................... 117
Finding Help ................................................... 119
Basic Principles ............................................... 121
Come ........................................................... 123
Sit-stay ....................................................... 127
Down-stay ...................................................... 132
Heel ........................................................... 136
Training Collars ............................................... 138
Stand For Petting .............................................. 140
Greeting ....................................................... 144
In Summary ..................................................... 146

# Chapter 7

SOCIAL SKILLS .................................................. 147
Be In Control:  Safety In Public ............................... 148
Be In Control:  Safety For The Dog ............................. 150
All Types Of People And Situations ............................. 151
Learn To "Read" People ......................................... 155
Courtesy In Public ............................................. 157
Put People At Ease ............................................. 158
Training In Public ............................................. 160

# Chapter 8

EXTRA CONTROL WORK AND HAND SIGNALS ......... 163
Training Signals ............................................... 164
Sit ............................................................ 164
Down ........................................................... 166
Heel ........................................................... 167
Come ........................................................... 168
Go Out, Take It, Go Say "Hi!" .................................. 168
Paws Up ........................................................ 170
Treats ......................................................... 171

Greetings: Shake Hands, Kiss, Nose, Head On Lap .. 173
Walking Skills: Wait, Easy, Move, Back, Side
And Go Through ............................................................ 175
Positions In Place ....................................................... 176
Front, Finish ................................................................ 177
Language ..................................................................... 180
Does Your Therapy Dog Need A Hobby? .................... 182
Tricks .......................................................................... 183

# Chapter 9

THE HANDLER'S JOB ...................................................... 185
Attitude ......................................................................... 186
Be Ready To Say No .................................................... 187
Water ............................................................................ 189
What To Wear ............................................................... 191
Times Of Day ................................................................ 192
Limits ............................................................................ 193
Attention On Dog, Potential Injuries ............................ 195
Zoonotic Diseases ....................................................... 200
Territorial Ranges - Space for Everyone ..................... 202
Handler As Interpreter ................................................. 211
What To Say On Your Visits ......................................... 213
The Handler Is The Key ................................................ 217
If The Dog Is Not A Registered Therapy Dog .............. 218

# Chapter 10

## Appendix 1

TEACHING A THERAPY DOG CLASS ............................. 219
Therapy Dog Training Begins ...................................... 220
Role-Playing ................................................................ 220
Assignment Behaviors for
"Friendly Stranger" Volunteers .................................... 222
Necessary Skills .......................................................... 222
Class One ..................................................................... 223
Class Two ..................................................................... 225
Class Three .................................................................. 225
Class Four .................................................................... 225
Class Five ..................................................................... 226
Class Six (Final) ........................................................... 227

## Appendix 2

THERAPY DOGS RESOURCES LIST ............................ 229
    National Therapy Dog Registries .................................. 229
    Human/Animal Bond Informational Resources ........... 230
    Internet Information Resources .................................... 230
    Resources for Information about Assistance Dogs for
    People with Disabilities ................................................. 231
    National Dog Trainer Organizations ........................... 232
    Dog Books ................................................................... 232
    Temperament Testing .................................................. 233
    Equipment And Supplies ............................................. 233
    Dog Magazines ............................................................ 235
    Contact the Author ...................................................... 236

**Appendix 3**

THERAPY DOGS ANNOTATED BIBLIOGRAPHY .......... 237

**Appendix 4**

FUN STUFF ................................................................. 245
ABOUT THE AUTHOR ................................................. 246

# Acknowledgments

To my dogs, Saint, Angel, Star, Spirit, Gabriel and Believer. Living with them has been a taste of heaven on earth.

To my husband, Bill, for support of every kind and for serving as the model handler for photographs.

To Linda O'Hare Newsome, for my wonderful Belgian Tervuren and for teaching me so much about training.

To Moira Allen, Seymour Weiss, the wonderful folks at Dogwise and Dr. Carolyn C. Hunt for help and encouragement.

My deep appreciation goes to all the people and families who generously allowed their photographs to be included, in order to provide readers with further insights into the world of therapy dog visits.

To God, for everything.

Kathy Diamond Davis

# INTRODUCTION

## AN UPDATE

It has been a privilege to update this second edition of *Therapy Dogs: Training Your Dog To Reach Others*. Therapy dog volunteers are some of the finest people I know, with the finest dogs. I wrote the book to be of service to these wonderful individuals. I am deeply grateful it has made a difference in so many lives.

Since the first edition, Saint, Angel and Star have completed their therapy dog careers. One at a time, with many tears, I held them in my arms as they left for heaven. Part of the heritage they left is what I can share with you in this second edition.

I have also adopted, raised and trained a puppy who turned out to have an unsuitable temperament for a therapy dog. Spirit, still by my side now as I write, has taught me as much as any of the dogs who have succeeded, and has added many insights to help choose and train therapy dogs.

For two years I taught a therapy dog class, until interest in my community had grown sufficiently for others to take over teaching. Therapy dog classes can fill the need for more volunteers in an area and provide vital support for handlers. This edition includes ideas for classes.

Finally, I have two new therapy dogs, Gabriel and Believer. They have added to my therapy dog training and handling education, lessons I am delighted to have the opportunity to share with you. Thank you for reading, and thank you for your interest in serving your fellow humans with your dog. May therapy dog work bring you as much joy as it has brought to my dogs and to me!

## THERAPY DOGS: A DEFINITION

Therapy dogs function to help people primarily in emotional ways, though physical benefits can result by boosting morale for physical therapy as well as self-care tasks. The term "therapy dog" was used by the first registry in the United States, **Therapy Dogs International,** for dogs taken on visits to health care facilities.

**Therapy Dogs Incorporated** and a number of other organizations have followed suit. **Delta Society** dogs are called "**Pet Partners.**"

"Animal-assisted therapy," "animal-assisted activity" and "pet therapy" are all terms that describe the encounter between a therapy dog and a person being visited. I use the term "therapy dog visit," which applies even when a licensed therapist is not involved. This book focuses on the job of the volunteer therapy dog handler. Many of us work along with licensed therapists on some visits, while on others we work without these paid professionals to provide benefits to people. Licensed professional therapists and counselors occasionally include dogs in their practice. See appendices for resources.

Therapy dogs have the right to go where they have been invited, including health-care facilities that, until the early 1980s, were legally off-limits to dogs. State by state in the United States—and in many other countries of the world—laws have been changed to provide this access for therapy dogs. It is state legislation rather than federal at this time.

It's essential to understand that a therapy dog is not an assistance dog. A dog that assists a person to function with a physical disability is in a different legal category, as well as a different functional one. Terms for these dogs include "assistance dog," "service dog," "hearing dog," "mobility assistance dog," "guide dog," and others. Assistance dogs for people with disabilities can also include dogs that alert to impending epileptic seizures, as well as a variety of other functions.

The **Americans with Disabilities Act** gives people with qualified disabilities the legal right to take their trained assistance dogs with them to places open to the public. One term for this is "public access rights." Therapy dogs are not included in the Americans with Disabilities Act and do not have federal public access rights under this legislation. State laws vary, and access rights in some states may apply to therapy dogs. It is important that therapy dog handlers not try to exercise public access rights inappropriately, because this behavior harms disabled people who need to exercise such rights with their assistance dogs.

This book will focus on practical instructions for managing, training and handling a therapy dog as part of a human-dog team. People seeking scientific data on therapy dog work can increasingly find it, because research in the field is ongoing. See the appendices for more information.

## A DISCLAIMER AND A NOTE ON STYLE

Careful reading of this book will inform the reader of the potential risks involved in therapy dog work and how to avoid them. Qualified handlers making therapy dog visits with trained dogs rarely cause accidents resulting in injury. Please realize, though, that the author cannot be held responsible for the actions or omissions of others working with therapy dogs. As in every other dog pursuit, each owner/handler must assume responsibility.

Many of the photos were taken by the author while working a dog on volunteer therapy dog visits, and copies were always given to the people pictured. They generally preferred to look at the camera and have the dog also facing the camera, for keepsake photos.

Language purists will notice the use of the word "person" when referring to patients, clients, children, participants, residents and others served by facility therapy dog visits. The term "patient" is considered unacceptable in many facilities when referring to the people receiving care. Such attention to terminology helps staff take seriously the needs, feelings and thoughts of the people they serve.

The term I have used in this book is "person," plural "people," in spite of the awkwardness in language it sometimes causes. The purpose of language is to serve people. Most of us prefer to be thought of as people first, not labeled according to a disability.

I also regret the necessity of referring to a dog as "it" when the dog could be of either sex. Be assured, I don't think of *any* dog as an "it." Due to the complexity of therapy dog interactions, I have to use pronouns to refer to the dog, the handler, the person being visited, the staff members, and the family members——I need to make sure you can tell which pronoun refers to the dog!

All photos are the work of the author unless otherwise credited.

*(Photo Credit, Bill Davis)*
*The author with her therapy dogs Saint, Angel and Star. Saint was Labrador/German shepherd, adopted from the city animal shelter at age 9 months. He retired from therapy dog work with lymphosarcoma at age 13 1/2 years, and went to heaven 11 months later. Angel was a miniature American Eskimo, adopted from the city shelter at age 18 months. She died after a short illness at two months short of 11 years, having served 7 1/2 years as a therapy dog. Star, a female Belgian Tervuren adopted from breeder Linda Newsome at age 7 months, died at 11 1/2 years of age after a 9 1/2 year therapy dog career.*

# 1

# BENEFITS THERAPY DOGS PROVIDE

Therapy dogs use their social instincts and learned social skills to bring people emotional benefits. Emotions are difficult to measure. Sometimes no one knows exactly how the dog helped, though they see positive changes in the person. Staff observations of the benefits, volunteer dedication to control and safety, and volunteers donating their services have made possible the great acceptance of therapy dog work.

This chapter will give volunteer therapy dog handlers an overview of how their dogs can help people. For more in-depth information, talk to facility staff about the therapeutic needs of the people they serve. Volunteers who regularly work their therapy dogs in facilities become part of the team.

## ORIENTATION TO REALITY

People are attracted to the sight of a dog. Filmmakers use this device frequently. Sometimes a dog moves across the screen for no other reason than to get you to look! If you walk with your dog, you have surely noticed how people are drawn to it. This helps people focus on the moment.

Some people with Alzheimer's disease, and other people whose minds wander, benefit from being brought mentally into the here and now as often as possible. The dog provides both a focal point and motivation. It can take a disoriented person some time to organize his or her thinking. The therapy dog handler may need to spend extra time with the person, or come back later in the visit.

## FOCAL POINT FOR ATTENTION-DEFICIT PROBLEMS

The same focal effect provides a benefit to children and others with learning disabilities. Many learning problems include the inability to concentrate. Until a person can concentrate, he or she can't learn. Think of the ability to concentrate as being like a muscle, gaining strength the more it is exercised. When the person focuses on the therapy dog longer than he or she can normally concentrate on any one thing, this "muscle" can become gradually stronger.

In some cases, the dog can also be used to help teach a child's lessons. A teacher might guide the child through specific material while you handle the dog as reward for the child's good work (example: child gets to toss ball for dog after solving a problem) or to help illustrate the lesson. Where a teacher doesn't set a specific goal, you and your dog can use retrieving and scent discrimination to help the children name colors, add numbers, spell words, and work on physical skills. The element of novelty is probably a factor, so part-time use of the dog, rather than at every session, may be most effective.

*Saint began therapy dog visits at age 7 1/2 years. Hyperactive as a young dog, he had lots to give when mature. This lady met him on his very first therapy dog visit, and made it easy for me to decide he was ready for the work.*

## MORALE

Keeping good morale in a facility is difficult. When the dog comes, morale invariably improves. I remember visiting an outpatient program for adults with emotional problems. When our therapy dog group arrived, people from the program were verbally picking on each other and making negative remarks. The change in the environment was electric by the end of the visit, with almost everyone behaving positively.

Staff members in facilities frequently mention improved morale for the rest of the day after a therapy dog visit. This benefit seems to apply to every type of facility therapy dogs serve.

## ANTIDOTE TO DEPRESSION

Therapy dogs help people overcome depression. Physical inactivity can bring on depression, as can having to move from your home. Life in a facility is routine. When the dog comes in, suddenly the day isn't boring.

A therapy dog is also a powerful antidote to handler depression! The physical exercise of taking care of a dog and training it, the touch involved in giving your dog its regular conditioning to handling, the emotional sense of connection to your neighborhood when you circulate with the dog to develop and maintain social skills, and the sure knowledge of the benefits you provide to your community through therapy dog visits will keep your spirits in excellent shape.

## COOPERATION

Increased cooperation between staff and the people receiving care endears therapy dogs to facilities. This happens partly because of improved morale and other factors. But you as a handler can facilitate it, through your manner when working the dog.

If you lovingly elicit good behavior from your dog instead of demanding it, you set a good example for staff as they deal with people. You aren't teaching them, because they already know how to treat people, but you make it easier to remember on difficult days. At the same time, your cooperative dog may inspire people to be more cooperative, too.

We aren't harsh and unfeeling toward our therapy dogs. Instead, we're loving partners. The handler is in charge, but just as a staff member sometimes takes charge when working with a person, being in charge is also a position of service. A good therapy dog handler and dog serve each other, as they work together to help people.

## SOCIAL STIMULATION

One reason therapy dog visits boost morale, alleviate depression and improve relationships among people is the social stimulation they provide. When you come in with the dog, people will talk to you, they'll talk to each other and they'll keep talking after you leave. If the facility is properly prepared for your visit, the talking will start before you come.

When you visit in meeting areas, social stimulation is increased by getting people together and out of their rooms. This process grows as people get to know the dog and begin coming out to

*Therapy dogs provide a powerful focal point for people of all ages in therapeutic interactions.  This young man enjoyed Saint's gentle kisses during sessions with his therapist.*

*One thing Saint and this terrific volunteer had in common:  both were great for morale in the daycare program for children with disabilities.*

see "their" dog. To leave their rooms, they may also get dressed and increase their physical activity, both positive behaviors. Staff members frequently look for ways to get people out of their rooms.

A mysterious and fascinating element adds to the ability of a dog to provide social stimulation. With multiple dogs in my house, I live constantly with dog language. I often hear and read about "animal ESP." I believe what people think of as extrasensory perception is normal sensory perception for dogs.

If you spend enough time with your dog and have a close bond, the dog will establish communication with you through its great skill with body language. Dogs have physical senses far more acute than human senses, so it's not hard to understand how these seemingly extra-sensory events occur. Dogs can communicate sophisti-cated information to percep-tive handlers, but it's only a small fraction of what our dogs are perceiving through their acute senses.

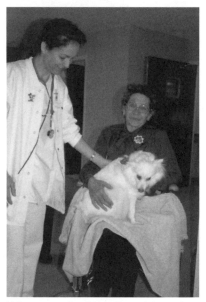

When my dogs chase a field mouse or other wild animal in the backyard, I in-terrupt them, never trusting the stray animal will escape. You see, it's not a simple matter of the animal running faster than the dogs. My dogs live together as a pack, with well-established lines of

*When people share thoughts and feelings about the therapy dog with staff, bonds of cooperation are strengthened.*

communication and rank. Like a pack of wolves when hunting for food, my dogs use intricate communication to tell each other "You go that way, I'll go this way. Stop and hold your position.

Get around on the other side," and much more. They send and receive these messages with lightning speed, faster than words. More than instinct is involved as dogs communicate and cooperate.

When people lose the ability or desire to speak for a while, it gets harder and harder to start again. Dogs are highly social animals. If you understand this about your therapy dog and provide it with the necessary opportunities to develop its social skills

*The social stimulation of coming out of their rooms to see the therapy dog can do people a world of good.*

with humans, your dog may actually learn to communicate with people that other people can't reach. Somehow this communication from the dog can help a person find a bridge back to speech. It can also help a child who's struggling against unusual difficulties in learning to speak for the first time.

One of the joys of handling a therapy dog is watching the dog communicate with other people. You can learn to read some of the signals, but probably never all of them. The two-way conversation never ceases to amaze me. This is perhaps the central reason to develop in your therapy dog the ability to work responsibly without tight control from you, i.e., the quality of initiative. Without it, you can't step back a pace and let your dog communicate as an individual with a person. With it you can watch, absorbed, as the subtle ballet goes on between dog and human, understanding enough of it to assist your dog when needed.

This ability as a handler will give you time to react when a potential problem develops. When you're good at reading people and dogs, you'll see potential trouble before it can happen. The more experienced the handler, the less risky therapy dog work becomes for the dog.

## NEED FOR TOUCH

Another way therapy dogs help people is by meeting the universal need for physical touch. This need isn't satisfied by the neutral touching involved in physical care, though many staff members give extra touch when they have time.

Some people receiving care in facilities have healthy relationships with relatives or caring staff people to provide needed touch. Others don't. Many of us are uncomfortable hugging or otherwise touching strangers, or even people we know. Sexual taboos can also make touch awkward. Therapy dogs enjoy the petting and hugging they get in their work. Their obvious enjoyment encourages more touch, bringing profound benefits to the people they visit.

Whole books have been written on the subject of touch for humans, and it is an extremely important subject when dealing with therapy dogs. Not only must the dog be conditioned to touch, but touch also plays a major role in nonverbal communication between people and dogs. The handler needs to know from lots of regular practice how to read these exchanges and when and how to intervene.

## SOCIALIZE CHILDREN TO DOGS

Another benefit therapy dogs can give is particularly relevant to children. Many children grow up without enough exposure to dogs to be able to relate to them in adulthood. Poor socialization of children to dogs, as well as poor education about dogs, leads to dog bites. These experiences can often be avoided or emotionally rehabilitated by a therapy dog team.

Children learn far more from a trained therapy dog and handler than from a dog at home no one has time to care for or train. With a therapy dog and handler, the child is never knocked down or bitten, and the child learns the best of dog behavior.

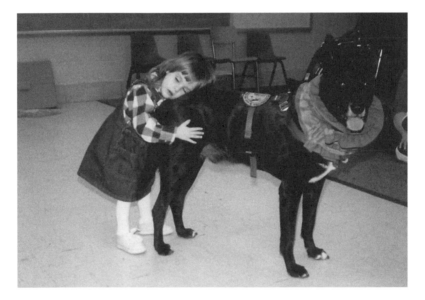

*This young girl met Saint when she was still a toddler. A guide dog will surely enhance her life as an adult. She learned dog body language, love and empathy for dogs, and respect for a dog's working ability with Saint's help. She even named her stuffed dinosaur after him!*

While education about dogs and gaining a positive image of dogs is important for people of any age, the most important period to learn this may end around age six. During the earliest years of life, children learn new languages, including dog language, with ease and develop lifelong social skills.

This benefit is also important for any child with a disability who might have a trained assistance dog partner later in life. He or she will need to be able to bond and communicate with a dog.

## WORKING WITH THERAPISTS

Therapy dog handlers often work directly with licensed therapists or other staff. In such cases, a professional leads the person toward specific therapeutic goals while the handler directs the therapy dog. You may get more feedback, and learn skills to help with all your therapy dog visits. Staff help also enables you to work with people you could not help on your own.

*Touch is a basic human need satisfied by therapy dogs. The dogs enjoy it, too! Sometimes people think they want to keep the dog, especially a cutie like Angel. True tales of the dog's mischief, and descriptions of the dog's care reminds people it might not be the best time in their lives to own a dog, but is a great time to enjoy the therapy dog's visit today.*

Generally, the therapy dog will be a special treat for the person receiving therapeutic services, and will not come to every session. Therapists will have sessions both with and without the dog, and will be able to tell you how the dog helps.

People tend to feel less tension when the dog is present. Instead of focusing on pain or frustration, they can focus on the dog. Therapy dogs improve morale and encourage people to work on therapy exercises. Therapy can be a long, difficult road. A dog is a great friend at such times.

## INCENTIVE

A therapy dog can serve as incentive. Time with the dog, going for a walk with the dog, or throwing a ball for the dog to retrieve will often induce people to cooperate with staff, exercise, come out of their rooms and otherwise participate in their own care.

## GETTING OUT OF YOURSELF

Staff can increase benefits to people through dog-related activities between therapy dog visits. People might draw pictures of dogs or have story-telling sessions to talk about their former pets. Groups might subscribe to dog publications or add dog books to the facility's library. People can watch dog shows on cable television.

Facilities can also involve people in gestures to encourage volunteers. Dinners, certificates and thank-you notes are common. People benefit therapeutically by helping with these expressions of thanks to the handler and dog. Such things also increase the therapy dog handler's commitment.

People gain therapeutic benefits from thinking of someone other than themselves. When my therapy dog Star was gravely ill at age three years, many of the people I visited with my other two therapy dogs prayed for her. We rejoiced together over her dramatic and full recovery.

*Ruby signed the sympathy card her facility sent to me when Angel died. It was healing for all of us. She treasured photographs like this one of her with Angel. Sometimes the photo will help bring someone with memory problems back into the moment. People often photograph better with a dog, because the dog relaxes them.*

After my therapy dog Angel died, one of the nursing homes she regularly visited sent a sympathy card, with signed notes from several of the residents. I think it helped them deal with their own grief, and I will treasure it forever. I came back to them with Star for the next scheduled visit.

Helping others alleviates depression and feelings of uselessness. Someone might help the dog experience a new piece of equipment in a relaxed or playful way. A nursing-home resident might invite the handler to sit and the dog to rest on the cool floor in a quiet room during a busy round of visits. A person might sincerely thank the handler for bringing the dog, and describe how much the people enjoy it. All of these actions allow a person to make a difference in the world by involvement with the therapy dog. We all need to be needed.

## PRACTICING PHYSICAL SKILLS

A therapy dog can help people work on specific physical skills. Some people benefit greatly from learning to handle a trained dog on its commands. If you don't wish to have your dog obey commands given by others, you can do playful interactions rather than commands. For example, my dogs catch or retrieve a tennis ball people throw for them, and they shake hands.

People healing in some types of facilities can walk dogs and benefit from the exercise. In many situations, the risk of some-one falling when walking the dog is unacceptably high. Giving the leash to another person can also cause undue stress on the dog. It's up to the handler to decide whether or not to allow someone else to take the leash. If you choose not to do this, and a specific facility wishes it for the people they serve, you can of course opt to serve elsewhere instead.

Shaking hands is a cue rather than a command, so people can work on this and be rewarded when the dog responds. If you choose to let people give treats to your dog on visits, they can use treats to elicit trick responses from the dog. Treats carry risks we will discuss later.

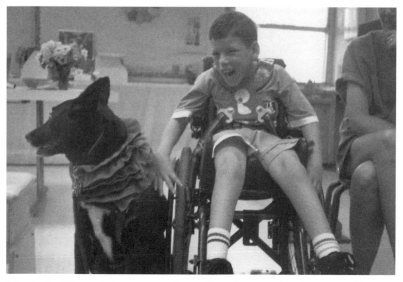

*Physical skills people can practice with a therapy dog include petting and throwing a tennis ball for the dog to retrieve. The handler can also walk a dog along with a person walking with a therapist, or station the dog for the person to walk toward it as a goal in therapy.*

## HAPPY ANTICIPATION

If the handler is dedicated, people benefit from happy anticipation of the coming visit. The more consistent you are, the more the staff will count on you and will prepare everyone for your visit. It's amazing how long it takes for your schedule to filter through to all the staff. You can make monthly visits for a year, and still have people who don't realize you come every month.

I find it useful to schedule visits for "the first Tuesday of every month," or similar designation. When a facility changes personnel, my visits are already on the schedule and are not interrupted. Personnel changes are frequent in some facilities, which is another reason the stability of regular therapy dog visits benefits people.

I cancel, or preferably reschedule, a visit if I'm sick, the roads are icy, or the dog is sick. I seldom make changes, and the facilities have learned to count on me. When staff can confidently tell people the therapy dog is coming, visits provide the benefit of anticipation.

It's generally best to schedule your visits back to any one facility no more often than once or twice a month. Handlers who visit the same facility weekly have a high rate of burnout. They often feel guilty when emotional stress causes them to quit in six months or so, and they consequently drop out with little closure for the people.

People get more attached to a particular dog when visits are weekly rather than with monthly visits, and may grieve when visits abruptly stop. A facility desiring weekly visits is better served by recruiting additional volunteers. Some people will respond more to one dog than to another anyway, plus the loss of one volunteer will not stop the entire program.

A volunteer desiring to make a weekly commitment will probably learn more and have a longer, more emotionally satisfying therapy dog career by spreading the commitment among two or more different facilities. Volunteers grieve when forced to give up visits to a facility after a long history there, too, and commitments to other facilities help buffer these emotional blows.

## EMOTIONAL SUPPORT TO STAFF AND FAMILY

I often work with staff members or family members of people in facilities. This might not seem to be the job of a therapy dog and handler, but sometimes it's vital. If you help a staff person, you help everyone the person's work touches. By helping someone's family member, you make it easier for the relative to continue to visit and care for the person. Visiting is less stressful for us as volunteers than it is for family members. It's much easier to maintain objectivity about an unpleasant remark someone makes out of ill health when the person is not your own mother or father.

*When the handler keeps appointments faithfully, staff can tell people the dog is coming and give them the benefit of happy anticipation. Here Star enjoys a nice back rub from an enthusiastic friend.*

# THERAPY DOGS

# 2

# WHAT KIND OF DOG?

Many therapy dog groups, local as well as national, set standards for their members. Criteria differ because the leaders have different ideas, and because the job is different in different situations. A dog and handler may be suited for some facilities and not for others. Each dog must be evaluated as an individual. The job of handling one dog can be radically different from the job of handling a different dog, even in the same breed. Handlers also have strong preferences about where they want to serve.

## BREEDS SUITED FOR THERAPY WORK

What breeds are best suited as therapy dogs? Well, first, we do not want to eliminate any individual dog that DOES qualify, just because many members of the breed would not. This is why therapy dog registries test each dog, and do not exclude any dog on the basis of breed. If we eliminate any dog without good reason, we eliminate help for those people who might respond only to a dog who reminds them of a dog they've known in the past. We may also eliminate a great volunteer in that dog's handler.

Some care facility programs will not allow specific breeds to participate, and some homeowners insurance companies will not cover your home if you own a dog of one of these breeds. This is a complication of dog ownership as well as therapy dog work that you need to understand before you adopt a dog of a breed that is going to make your legal status more complicated. I do not endorse this position on the part of various entities, but some of them are making these choices.

In considering any breed for a therapy dog, talk to the guardians of that breed. You will find both national breed club contact information and rescue contact information for each breed listed on the AKC website, www.akc.org. These people deeply care about their breeds, and are highly motivated to tell you the truth about any difficulties you might experience with each breed in therapy dog work.

Every therapy dog should be, foremost, someone's beloved companion dog. If you have your heart set on a certain breed, and your dog turns out unsuited for therapy dog work, who's to say you made the wrong choice, really, for yourself?

Let me emphasize again, there are dogs from nearly EVERY breed serving magnificently as therapy dogs. If you are in love with a particular breed, responsible breeders in that breed can help you find an individual dog with the best chance of success as a therapy dog. A properly selected dog of a "difficult" breed will be a better choice, absolutely, than a poorly selected dog of a breed that everyone considers a "natural" therapy dog! Don't place excessive emphasis on the dog's breed in selecting a therapy dog. It's the individual dog that matters.

What about mixed breeds? Provided the dog is an adult when selected, this can be an excellent choice. A mixed-breed puppy is a big gamble, since it may grow up with health or temperament problems from either or both sides of its parentage that are not visible when you select the puppy.

The single most important factor is matching your handling ability with the dog's traits. That starts with choosing a dog you want to live with, because this is going to be your dog. The better your relationship with your dog as companions, the greater your potential will be as a therapy dog team.

Small dogs are easiest for beginners to handle, but should work only with people who won't treat them too roughly. There are some facilities in which you simply will not work a small dog, and others where you may need to keep a small dog out of some people's reach. In the right situations, a small dog can be an outstanding therapy dog.

With a large dog, control becomes more of an issue. It's ideal if the dog is no stronger than the handler. Working a dog you can physically restrain without a special collar simplifies both training and handling on visits, and adds an extra margin of safety. To match your strength, the dog would weigh no more than one-third of what you weigh. By this standard, a small woman can handle a dog big enough to work with all groups. With enough training, though, a small person can handle a large dog; it's done all the time. The larger the dog, the more training both handler and dog need.

Now for the question of male dogs versus female dogs. Aggressiveness tends to be somewhat higher in male dogs than in females, but this varies greatly by breed. Even docile male dogs can become targets for attack by other males. Many male dogs make fine therapy dogs, especially if neutered by about one year of age, as are male dogs in assistance work. Male dogs may be more extroverted, which in some breeds will be an advantage.

In general, female dogs are more obedient than males of the same breed, but this difference is so small in some breeds that it is insignificant. A female dog should not go on a therapy dog visit when she is in heat, and the variation in cycles can complicate the handler's job of being faithful to the schedule for therapy dog visits. Having her spayed will eliminate this disadvantage, of course.

Either sex can make a great therapy dog, provided the dog is carefully managed, properly supported on visits by the handler, and appropriately screened for the work. Therapy dog registries do not require that you spay or neuter your dog in order to do therapy dog visits.

## CHOOSING A PUPPY FOR THERAPY DOG WORK

Many people adopting dogs insist on puppies. One trait, or perhaps it should be thought of as a constellation of traits, important in therapy dog work is defensiveness. This trait usually begins to emerge around the time of puberty. A dog high in defensiveness may panic under stress, depending on other factors in the dog's temperament. Even if training helps, the dog may always feel more stress with strangers than if it were less defensive by nature.

A dog high in defense drives can make a good therapy dog if it is not easily triggered to a defensive response, if its reactions are completely under the handler's control, and if the dog recovers quickly. Training, socialization and the right handler will maximize the dog's ability. None of this can be evaluated in a puppy.

Besides a defensive temperament, a puppy may later develop physical health problems not evident in puppyhood. Severe skin allergies, hip dysplasia and other common medical conditions often represent obstacles to therapy dog work. Broken skin from allergies makes a dog's skin unsuited to be presented to people for petting, and hip dysplasia can cause pain to the dog when it walks on slick floors or is petted on the hindquarters by people. The mental and physical make-up of a dog is altogether more apparent at a year or so of age than it is in puppyhood.

Temperament testing for puppies can be of some help with your choice. Breeders commonly administer some standard tests. You can try these out with puppies you have not previously met. Remove the puppy from the littermates, from other dogs, and from the puppy's familiar territory for the most accurate results. The test area should be clean and enclosed.

When the pup has had a short time to explore the area, squat down and call the puppy to you with an exciting voice, patting your legs with your hands, etc. The puppy that happily comes to you is showing a nice reaction for a therapy dog, provided it does not wildly nip at your fingers or nose!

Walk around and see if the puppy follows you. Calmly following without too much grabbing at your shoelaces or pants legs is a good response.

Using an object easy for the puppy to hold (crumpled paper, a light-weight dog toy, a sock with a knot in it, etc), get down on the puppy's level and toss the toy where the puppy can track with its eyes. If the puppy runs out and picks it up, that's a nice sign, and even nicer if the puppy runs back to you with it. Retrieving instinct is not essential for therapy dog work, but it's helpful.

Get down on the puppy's level again, and restrain it gently on its back. If the puppy struggles a bit, but generally accepts the restraint, that's a good sign for a therapy dog. If a puppy does not wiggle at all, that's not necessarily good. You should retest that puppy at a different time. Equally important is what the puppy does when released. The desired reaction is for the puppy to still want to be with you.

Sensitivity to touch can be important in a therapy dog. To test this, nestle the pup into a seated position, and gently take a front paw in your hand. Press the webbing between two of the toes between your thumb and forefinger, being very sure your fingernails apply no pressure. Start softly and steadily increase the pressure, while you count silently from one to ten.

Stop at the first sign the puppy wants you to stop, by fussing or trying to pull the paw away. Some dogs are a "1" on this test. While some highly touch-sensitive dogs do function well as therapy dogs, it is a disadvantage that would need to be compensated by other traits and training. The best candidate would be the dog with a high number.

If you have your heart set on raising your own puppy, you need to be willing to accept it turning out unsuited as a therapy dog. This commonly happens, in spite of careful breeding and skilled puppy testing. My dog Spirit's puppy tests were absolutely perfect for therapy dog criteria. She followed humans, came when called, was moderate on touch sensitivity, no fear of noises, retrieved naturally, and showed no dominance with other dogs or humans. But as defense drives and other problems emerged, it became clear she was unsuited. When therapy dog work is your top priority, you will want to seriously consider adopting an adult dog rather than a puppy. Police dogs, assistance dogs and other working dogs go to their owners after puberty, and still form the strongest possible bonds.

## SOURCES FOR YOUNG ADULT DOGS

One excellent source for young adult dogs with good puppy training is the dog fancier. When a carefully socialized and trained competition puppy doesn't grow tall enough or has some other conformation flaw or competition disadvantage unrelated to good health or temperament, placing the young adult dog with an active therapy dog handler can give it a good home and a productive life. This was Gabriel's situation. He is too short for the conformation ring, but a perfect size for me as a therapy dog.

*Therapy dogs Gabriel, Max and Sasha all came to their homes as adults, not as puppies. Max and Sasha served as therapy dogs in the aftermath of the Murrah Building bombing here in Oklahoma City, while Gabriel came to live with me that same week.*

Animal shelters and other sources such as rescue groups also contain good prospects for therapy dog work. The more known about the dog's history, the better. A dog in a shelter is likely to be tired and stressed. At least two weeks of careful evaluation in a foster home can help determine whether the dog has potential as a therapy dog.

Qualifying with your dog for therapy dog work is truly an on-going process. A reason to remove your dog from service can arise at any time. Evaluation by a therapy dog organization will help you make an objective decision. If at any time you believe your therapy dog could no longer pass the evaluation, it's time to withdraw the dog from service. Keep training up to date. Plan ahead for your next dog. A therapy dog may have to retire quite unexpectedly, and a skilled therapy dog handler without a therapy dog to take on visits is a sad loss to everyone concerned.

## TRAINABILITY

In whatever facility you choose to visit, you must be able to control your dog at all times. That's a tall order, and all therapy dogs and their handlers need training in control work. This training includes commands to come-when-called, sit-stay, down-stay, and walk on a loose leash.

Therapy dogs work on leash most of the time, but training for off-leash control greatly increases the margin of safety. A leash can slip off, and other emergencies or handling situations can arise. On leash as well as off leash, training the dog to take commands is of no use unless the handler is also trained to handle the dog skillfully.

Control training gives handlers confidence and an understanding of their own and their dogs' limitations. Good training calms sassy dogs and nervous dogs alike, while building a stronger bond between handler and dog. To bring a dog to a level of solid training usually takes at least six months. The dog must be a year old before formal evaluation, since the full temperament is not apparent prior to this. It will take much longer with some dogs. It takes as long as it takes, and rushing it will not work.

## SOMEBODY'S BABY

One special quali-fication of a therapy dog is what I call be-ing "somebody's baby." If you haven't had experience with this work, you might think a dog attached to its owner wouldn't make a good therapy dog. The opposite is true. Just as a child needs loving parents or someone early in life to give deep and uncon-ditional love to grow into an adult who can love others, a dog who will serve the public as a therapy dog needs loving support at home.

*The match between dog and handler is the single most important factor in therapy dog work. A close relationship is the foundation.*

Interacting with friendly strangers is a job the dog learns, with the handler's help. A strong bond with the handler teaches the dog how to relate to a human, makes it possible for the dog to work under the handler's control, and gives the dog confidence.

A strong bond also allows the handler to work the dog in a loving model for how others will treat the dog. When the handler relates to the dog with obvious love, everyone is assured the dog is loved and is safe at home. This greatly adds to the effectiveness of therapy dog visits.

## BENEFITS TO THE DOG

Many dogs need jobs. With the right training, the same types of dogs guiding the blind, assisting people in wheelchairs and alerting deaf people to important sounds also make excellent therapy dogs. These types of dogs need the responsibility and pride of work. Serving as a therapy dog can satisfy such needs.

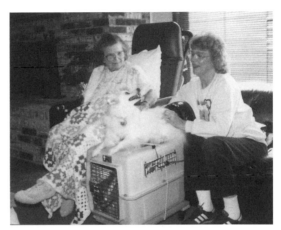

*From the moment I told her on the morning of each visit "Angel gets to go, yes, GO!" Angel loved everything about her therapy dog visits.*

Other dogs aren't working dogs in this sense. They were bred to be pets, or for tasks like pest control without human direction. Some dogs won't enjoy therapy dog work, and certainly shouldn't be forced into it. In most breeds there are at least a few highly sociable dogs that would be happier with extra people to love. Their styles in therapy dog work may be quite different from the styles of more work-oriented breeds, but equally beneficial to the people they serve.

A therapy dog gets to go on visits and socialization outings. A therapy dog also gets more invitations to accompany you with family and friends, because others know the dog will behave. The dog gets to spend more time with you because of its beautiful manners and enjoyment of other people. Therapy dog training is gentle and fun for the dog. The dog has a more interesting life.

## BENEFITS TO THE HANDLER

The benefits to the handler include all the benefits to the dog and more. The extra outings with your dog are a huge benefit. Some people satisfy this desire through dog shows and other events with the goal of earning titles on the dog. Unlike most such events, therapy dog work is noncompetitive. People will compliment your well-trained and well-groomed dog, and thank you repeatedly for coming.

*Unlike dog shows, therapy dog work happens in quiet places, quiet moments. Few dogs win every show, but on every therapy dog visit the therapy dog wins, when people call the dog beautiful and marvel at its training. And on every therapy dog visit, the dog and handler make a difference in people's lives.*

Therapy dog visits do not require entry fees like dog shows, and you may even be able to deduct mileage to and from therapy dog visits on your income tax as a charitable contribution. You may also have lower veterinary expenses than when showing dogs. Contaminated show grounds and dogs brought long distances expose dogs to disease. Therapy dogs can work close to home, around few other dogs, in clean conditions.

Dog shows help owners enjoy their dogs and learn more about them. Performance events maintain and improve the abilities of working breeds. Many people choose to spend a major part of their lives in these pursuits. They will always be essential to therapy dog work, because dog competitions are a major system for responsible breeding and training and for the training of new handlers.

Most people who take dogs through obedience classes don't go on to earn obedience titles or compete in agility events. They want well-behaved dogs, but aren't interested in competition or breeding. Some of these handlers and their dogs are excellent candidates for therapy dog work.

## COMPETITION vs THERAPY DOG WORK

Other prospects for therapy dog work are the many people who participate in competitive events for several years before deciding to stop. I was one of these. I find therapy dog work more satisfying. The more competition enthusiasts know about therapy dog work, the more therapy dog volunteers can come from this large number of well-educated dog people who, along with their trained dogs, find themselves "all dressed up and no place to go."

Conflicts between therapy dog work and competitions force some dog owners to choose one or the other:
1. Therapy dogs have distinct advantages when neutered. Conformation show dogs can't be shown or bred after being neutered.
2. Dog showing carries with it an obligation to support clubs and events, a serious time commitment. Therapy dog

work also involves a serious time commitment, and there is only so much time!

3. The training for therapy dog work is different from any form of competition training. Some handlers and dogs will easily combine two or more pursuits, but others will find part or all of their work suffers.

4. During competition season, it may be impossible for serious competitors to keep up therapy dog visits. To make regular visits for part of the year until people get attached and staff gets into a routine, and then drop out for the season, is not the best way to serve the needs of therapy dog work.

5. In the conformation ring, the dog needs to stand like a beautiful statue when the judge approaches. A therapy dog needs to exhibit expressive body language when it meets people. One trick to keeping the show dog's ears up when the judge approaches is for people in the dog's daily life not to pet the dog on the top of the head, which causes a dog to lower the ears. A therapy dog will be petted on top of the head on visits, and needs conditioning to this approach so as not to find it intimidating.

*Therapy dog work is different from any other dog job, and requires different training. Conditioning the dog for gentle responses with people requires consistent direction in all the dog's training and conditioning to handling.*

6. The competition dog must obey commands reflexively and without

pausing to think, in order to have a chance of winning. The therapy dog needs to think about each command, not respond reflexively. The instant response of the competition dog could be dangerous in a facility where there are hazards the handler may fail to see before giving a command. The therapy dog must consistently remain aware of the environment.

I'm not suggesting people who participate in competitive events with their dogs shouldn't work with therapy dogs. On the contrary, I think clarifying these issues can help dog fanciers participate in therapy dog work. Dog people are great problem solvers!

Dog fanciers who are not able to participate extensively in individual therapy dog visits are instrumental in educational and entertainment programs. They help recruit new therapy dog handlers by encouraging people who don't plan to compete or who retire from competing to consider this work. They place young, retired competition dogs with experienced therapy dog handlers. They train handlers who don't own dogs to work retired dogs on therapy dog visits, while the dogs continue living with their owners. This is a great way to make use of your dog expertise, to train new therapy dog handlers, and to give added meaning to the lives of retired dogs.

I hope this book will serve obedience instructors wishing to learn about therapy dogs. It is a different form of training than for any other job involving dogs. One of the greatest benefits to the therapy dog handler is the joy to be found in the training. Therapy dog work provides many of us with the deep satisfaction of working with a dog as a true partner.

Obedience-trial enthusiasts can promote special classes to serve therapy dog handlers. Such classes need to differ from classes for competitive obedience. Dog clubs and private instructors who teach good skills classes for therapy dogs and their handlers will find themselves much in demand, since the training suits family dogs as well.

## BENEFITS TO THE COMMUNITY

Therapy dog handlers work regularly on social skills in public. The public helps train therapy dogs by petting them, as opposed to the problem created when the public distracts dogs assisting disabled people by petting them.

In most communities, proprietors don't have to let therapy dogs enter. Trained dogs assisting people with disabilities have public access rights by federal law, but therapy dogs do not. Restaurants, grocery stores and airplane cabins are not necessary for therapy dog training, since they are not settings where therapy dogs work. Handlers build relationships based on trust with proprietors of businesses where dogs are not prohibited by law. In the process, the public gains valuable insight into the proper way to care for and control a dog.

Therapy dog handlers have a wonderful opportunity to demonstrate practical and humane dog handling to the public. People benefit from experiencing the body language, tone of voice, timing and good attitude of a truly skilled dog handler.

*When therapy dogs and handlers circulate in the community to practice social skills, people are exposed to a level of dog care and training they might otherwise never see.*

Area children benefit from having a therapy dog in the neighborhood. Working parents and city living combine to prevent many children from growing up with a well-managed family dog. When neighborhood children pet therapy dogs, handlers fulfill an important need for these families. Therapy dogs and their owners show neighbors a standard of proper dog care and control they might not otherwise experience.

## WHAT IF YOU DON'T HAVE A DOG

Getting a new dog is not the first action for you to take. Working with a therapy dog is a complex handling skill. It also requires excellent care and management of the dog at all times. It's easy to adopt a dog. Don't give in to the temptation to acquire a dog hastily, before you have properly prepared.

*Michelle had no dog, and Marilyn Smith, owner of retired conformation champion and obedience-titled Candy, wasn't able to find time for regular therapy dog visits. Marilyn trained Michelle with Candy at home and in obedience class until the two were ready to team on therapy dog visits. Armed with much more knowledge and skill, Michelle eventually got her own Labrador.*

So how do you start? First, if you own a dog you don't think is suited, seek skilled advice. You may need to change the way you care for and work with your dog, and go through a training course. There may be nothing "wrong" with your dog.

Whether you own a dog or not, seek out local handlers who work with therapy dogs. Observe some visits. Offer your services as a volunteer. Your presence on the visit can make a contribution right from the start. I wish I had an extra person to help on every visit! You may receive valuable experience with a trained dog whose owner has more available therapy dogs than time to visit. If and when the dog's owner feels you're ready, you may be able to take the dog on therapy dog visits, or the owner may bring it for you to handle while he or she works another dog. At some point you'll be ready to select a dog for yourself.

If you are a therapist or an activities or social service professional in a facility or in private practice, and are thinking about becoming a therapy dog handler, here are some issues to consider. Would it be emotionally healthy for you to spend your free time volunteering in the same setting where you spend your working hours? Or, do you want to try to handle a dog and work with clients at the same time? Would clients then get your full attention? Would your dog have your total focus as a handler? Can you arrange for the dog to have some hours of undisturbed rest during the day if you bring it to work with you? What about the additional liability incurred when therapy dog services are part of paid care provided by a facility or independent professional? Health-care professionals can work with volunteer therapy dog handlers before taking any steps toward becoming handlers themselves. Many professionals continue using volunteers indefinitely.

## PUBLICITY

You've probably seen news articles and television stories about therapy dogs. Unfortunately, much of the media coverage doesn't represent the work accurately. Faithful therapy dog handlers work in quiet situations, seldom in the limelight. A therapy dog visit is not a show, although it may be entertaining. Handlers educate, but we work largely with people who can't have dogs themselves and have no money to donate to dog charities.

Therapy dog visits are often unexciting to watch. Some benefits to people are seen in the flicker of a hand, an eye or the corner of a mouth. It's a quiet, controlled activity, boring to uninformed observers. Most of the miracles are simple. Even the exciting results are often understood only by someone familiar with the person's medical history. Frequently the handler is never even told how the dog helped. Those seeking publicity for dog activities will find entertainment and educational programs much more productive than therapy dog work.

## THE INDOOR DOG

The best place for a therapy dog to live is in the house. This requires commitment from the owner. A dog living in the house learns how to behave indoors with people, not to relieve itself indoors, and how to tone down behavior. A housedog drools less.

*Most therapy dog work takes place away from exciting publicity. No longer a novelty, therapy dog visits are seldom considered "newsworthy" events to attract publicity for dog organizations.*

A dog's respiratory system actually changes after the dog spends as little as two weeks in a climate-controlled place. Drooling less is a big benefit for a therapy dog, but a disadvantage for dogs that work outdoors: it reduces the dog's ability to cool itself and can impair its stamina.

Housedogs usually learn to walk on slick floors. If your house is completely carpeted or if your dog lives outdoors, seek out places for the dog to play on vinyl flooring, ceramic tile and other slick surfaces regularly. You will encounter such floors in most facilities, and therapy dogs must not fear them. Similarly, if your house has no stairs, find some to use for practice.

When my grandparents ran a household, most people lived in rural communities. Farm dogs like Mud, my grandmother's working German shepherd, got dirty every day. People didn't have today's products for parasite control. Farm families spent much of their time outdoors with their dogs. Mud slept outside my grandmother's bedroom window, which went all the way to the floor, so he could be near her at night.

Mud's heritage lives on in my dogs, but I'm a city dweller. I pick up my yard every day, and my dogs aren't dirty. I keep my house and yard free of fleas and ticks. There's no reason for my dogs to have to watch over me through the bedroom window at night. They belong beside me.

This depicts a typical change in families. Previous generations living in largely rural communities kept dogs outdoors for good reasons irrelevant to today's city dogs. They knew dogs as trainable, working animals. Today many dogs live indoors in order to do their jobs as life-extending companions to humans, and to keep dog-related complaints from neighbors to the minimum. Training your dog, and using the training every day, will let you live happily with an indoor dog. A therapy dog must be clean and well behaved enough for its owner's home before going into facilities where other people live and work.

*Fleas, ticks, worms and other potential health hazards to humans are unthinkable in therapy dogs. It is ideal for the dog to be an immaculately-kept housedog, ready to go into the squeaky-clean residences and indoor facilties used by other people.*

## PARASITE CONTROL

Therapy dogs must never carry fleas or ticks into a facility. The only practical solution is to consistently control fleas and ticks at home. Consult your veterinarian about pest control for your geographical area. Follow your veterinarian's directions exactly, since improper use of pesticides can kill your dog.

Wormers are just as dangerous as flea and tick products when used incorrectly. If your dog has worms, let your veterinarian prescribe the wormer and the dosage. It's not worth the risk of killing your dog to save a little money.

Proper management of a dog means picking up dog feces in your yard every day. Pick up after the dog if it uses property outside your yard, too. This is the only way to avoid the risk of contaminating the soil. You might not know your dog has worms or an infection for quite some time. If you pick up every day, you greatly reduce the risk of transmitting problems to another dog or reinfecting your own dog after treatment.

The most convenient way to pick up is to put a plastic bag over your hand like a glove, pick up, invert the bag over the feces and discard. Since handlers also have to be prepared to pick up after their dogs on outings and at facilities, this is an essential skill to learn.

If you can't clean every day, do it without fail at least once a week. Still, this turns a simple job into a big one, and means a dirty yard between cleanings. When the yard is not picked up, the family gets less use of the area, the dog has less room to exercise and it will be hard for the dog to avoid the mess. Then you won't want the dirty dog in the house, and you'll have a big job cleaning the dog before taking it on therapy dog visits.

## THE VETERINARIAN

Visits to the veterinarian allow you to practice handling skills for when your dog is under stress and feeling mild pain. Working with the dog when discomfort is inevitable for the dog's benefit is the only humane way for you to practice these skills. Inflicting pain on a dog for practice would damage your dog's confidence in you. Testing a dog by having others inflict pain on it could ruin the dog's trust in other people.

Don't expect to fool a dog, with its keen senses and ability to read body language, into thinking an intentional act was an accident. A dog will often recognize painful episodes on a therapy dog visit as purely accidental. Pain and fear in the veterinary setting is also unintentional. Handling your dog during routine veterinary procedures is an opportunity to observe your dog's responses and learn what handling from you most supports your dog.

If you have a huge dog, you may not be able to hold it alone, and it may need to be attended to on the floor. For a smaller dog to receive care on the table, you can use both arms to hold the dog in a standing position. Wrap one arm around the dog's belly from underneath and the other around the dog's neck from underneath. Hold the dog against your body, and reach each hand as far around as you can, to keep the dog's head from turning back and to hold the dog steady. If necessary, encircle the dog's muzzle with your hand at the head. When possible, use the hand to scratch the dog behind its ears vigorously, which reduces sensations of pain elsewhere on the dog's body. Talk to the dog in a steady, pleasant voice to hold its focus.

Pay close attention to how your dog reacts to pain and fear, and be honest about it. Your veterinarian handles lots of dogs and can give you a skilled opinion, too. If your dog goes out of control when it feels pain or fear, it shouldn't be a therapy dog.

Holding your dog at the veterinarian's office is valuable practice. Here Bill supports Star in a standing position, with the arm around her neck leaving a hand available to scratch her ears as he keeps her attention with an interesting voice.

Carry treats to the veterinarian's office, and encourage the doctor and assistants to use them. Let your dog get the treats from them, if possible. If your dog snaps at food, tell attendants in advance so they can offer treats safely from the palms of their hands. You will likely find the veterinarian pleased to help with this, since it will make your dog easier to deal with in the future. Start the treats before anything uncomfortable happens, as well as after, in order to orient the dog's attention to something pleasant. Use small pieces of easy-to-digest food. If you forget, your veterinarian may have treats on hand.

With permission from the veterinarian, take your dog along on trips to the office when it won't be examined at all.  Go when the office is quiet, not when your dog would be exposed to sick dogs or when your visit might be disruptive.  These trips help condition the dog not to fear the place.

Therapy dog owners are not average dog owners.  Your veterinarian will get to know you and how you manage your dog.  After you develop a good working relationship, you'll be able to perform some care at home under the veterinarian's instructions, which will save you money.

Your dog will have serious medical problems once in a while, and then a good veterinarian is your best ally.  Some major medical problems will eliminate your dog from therapy dog work, while others won't.  Get your veterinarian's help in deciding.  Some illnesses require isolation, or make the dog pain-sensitive or irritable.  In these cases a therapy dog must not work.

Your therapy dog, male or female, will benefit from being neutered.  Sexual relations don't mean the same things to dogs as to people.  Dogs are commonly able to live happily together in social units because of being neutered.  Neutering allows your male or female dog to respond to you more consistently, especially in the presence of other dogs. It does not deprive your dog of its personality or sexual identity, but does provide the dog with many health benefits.  Don't hesitate to have your dog neutered; you're doing it a favor.

At some point an aging therapy dog may have to retire.  Some dogs can visit until the end of their lives; no one can predict.  Watch the older dog for reduced tolerance of handling, and for increased body sensitivity.  With any medical condition, you need to specifically ask your veterinarian if the dog should still be making therapy dog visits.  Don't leave it to the veterinarian to remember and to bring up this sensitive subject.  When the dog no longer enjoys visits, or begins to create health risks to people, it's time to stop.

You'll need to learn about health care continually from your veterinarian, from other dog owners and from dog publications. It takes time and effort to learn how to provide the excellent care a therapy dog needs.

## IS THERAPY DOG WORK FOR YOU?

This is a good time to stop and think about what it means to be a therapy dog handler and whether it's what you want. Is this the way you want to live with your dog?

Dogs and people both become awkward with others if they stay alone too much, which is one reason therapy dogs help people. You can't just train your dog and have it stay permanently trained. You must practice throughout the dog's career to keep up both its skills and yours. It's a way of life.

Some people don't enjoy initiating social interaction with strangers. Your dog will be an enormous help in this, but you'll be the leader. If you don't like interacting with strangers, you might never enjoy being a therapy dog handler. Ask yourself whether this work fits your personality.

Handling a therapy dog requires a certain amount of talent and skill. Every therapy dog deserves the protection of a good handler. If handling a therapy dog is not one of your abilities or interests, there are many other ways you can help therapy dog work. If you are a professional in a health-care facility, you can help to establish a program in the facility with volunteers and their dogs. If you own or manage a public place where health codes do not prohibit dogs, you can invite qualified therapy dog handlers to bring their dogs in regularly for social skills practice. If you produce stories for the news media, you can represent therapy dog work accurately. If you want to participate in therapy dog visits, you can go along to help stimulate people socially. If you are a veterinarian, you can give good advice to facilities and handlers, and arrange funding for any special tests facilities require on therapy dogs. If you teach obedience classes, you can spot, encourage and give special help to dog owners who want to learn therapy dog work. If you belong to a dog club, you can arrange classes and tests for therapy dogs and their handlers. If you live near a therapy dog handler, you can offer to help with training.

While handling a therapy dog is not for everyone, everyone has a role to play in providing therapy dog service to those who need it. Chances are you'll find your part a welcome addition to your life.

*You're likely to enjoy therapy dog work if you take genuine pleasure in helping your dog give love to others.*

# THERAPY DOGS

# 3

# VISITS AS A GROUP

## THE RIGHT FACILITY FOR YOU AND YOUR DOG

How do you decide which facilities to serve with your dog? First you train with your dog and become a smooth team. You need to know your dog's capabilities as well as your own. We all have limits! You also need to know your dog's likes and dislikes, and to honestly assess your own as well.

Don't be unduly influenced by the settings you might see most often in the news. When possible, the media loves to show an adorable child with a therapy dog. Working a therapy dog with children is much more difficult than you might think. Children under school age need to interact with the dog in small groups, preferably three or fewer but never more than five, with alert, skilled adult management for the kids. The therapy dog handler will need to be right there for the dog, focused, supportive, and highly skilled. The dog needs to be quite comfortable with kids. It's best to gain other therapy dog experience before taking an assignment in a facility with young children. Little children leap around, squeal, bop the dog on the head, fall over the dog, pull the tail and ears, get right into a dog's face, etc. Of course the person handling the kids is supposed to control all this!

Being a parent yourself would seem to be an additional asset for therapy dog visits to children, but some parents find it too emotionally stressful to visit sick, injured or disabled children. For a parent, it can be overwhelming to think "What if this were my child?" This reaction can occur in any therapy dog setting that strikes too close to your personal situation. Don't let it stop you from doing therapy dog work, but you certainly will want to consider choosing a venue that allows you a bit of healthy emotional space.

School-age children are easier for dog and handler to work with, and you can usually interact with larger groups, provided none of the kids have disabilities that involve violence. With this or any other group where violence could be an issue, you need to carefully consider your own temperament as well as that of your dog. Therapy dog work is not the appropriate place for a dog to exercise protection behavior! You want the dog to feel safe, and to believe there is no need for defense. This is achieved by making sure skilled staff is always present to handle people who might require it. Your dog can then learn to trust the staff to control the people, and to trust you to immediately put a stop to any dangerous interaction.

Psychiatric facilities also have the potential for aggressive gestures toward the dog. Whenever you feel a situation might be too much for your dog or for you, arrange to go and observe first without your dog. The most intense situations are those that include violence. Other difficult settings include those where people are both highly mobile AND confused. People with Alzheimer's Disease at certain stages can fit this category.

Hospice care is a wonderful opportunity to be of service with your therapy dog. You should be aware of the emotional investment involved, since you will likely be called upon to visit the person weekly, and to cope with having the person die after you have spent a lot of time together.

You will also need to decide whether or not to do home visits. Potential concerns here include possibly a resident pet that would not appreciate the intrusion of your therapy dog. Another issue is whether or not you are willing to be alone with a person at home. Having someone else present during your therapy dog visits would help avoid such concerns as the dog later being accused of having harmed someone, with no witness to the actual visit. You might find yourself in care situations for which you are not prepared. A therapy dog handler's job is to focus on the dog. Providing other services to the person inevitably means taking focus off your job of handling the dog.

An exciting possiblity is to support children and other vulnerable people through the process of police and courtroom questioning when they have been witnesses or victims of crimes.

Hospitals are a popular visitation option with therapy dog handlers, and contain a variety of settings. Rehabilitation units can be inside or outside of a hospital, and generally are enjoyable visitation opportunities where you will have good staff support. Each unit in a hospital has different problems and therefore is likely to have different rules concerning therapy dogs. You may encounter some rules that don't make any sense, because hospitals tend to be somewhat bureaucratic. Such rules might include requirements that all therapy dogs wear clothing too hot for your particular dog. Sometimes the solution is to patiently work to change an unworkable rule, while at other times the best idea is to transfer to a different unit in the hospital, or to a different type of facility.

Nursing homes and other long-term care facilities have a great need for therapy dogs, and tend to be some of the most welcoming venues. Keep assisted-living centers and other settings that serve older people in mind, too.

Some schools have programs where therapy dogs are a good fit. There is a great need for dog education programs in the schools, sometimes including entertainment. These may or may not be therapy dog visits, depending on the students being served.

If you want to help people dealing with the criminal justice system, take the time to patiently work through police, district attorneys, and other officials to earn their trust in you and your dog.

For handlers available on weekdays during the day, various day programs are eager for therapy dog visits. Adult day care, day care for children with disabilities, rehabilitation institutes, and facilities providing a wide variety of services that are delivered during workdays are all possibilities. I would love to serve in waiting rooms, comforting people with my therapy dog while they wait for medical services they or their loved ones are receiving. This is a task I don't think many therapy dog teams are doing, but it appeals to me, and seems a place we could be of great service.

The first step is to train with your dog. Keep training until you are a team, go through therapy dog testing, and gain experience on group visits with an established therapy dog visitation program. After that, if you want to explore other possibilities, start making phone calls and perhaps even in-person inquiries. Learn about the new setting, fulfill necessary requirements, and come in with the right skills to demonstrate the usefulness of therapy dog work in a new place. There are plenty of new frontiers for therapy dog handlers to explore!

## DISASTER WORK

In light of developments since September 11th, 2001, there has been an increased interest in the use of therapy dogs in disaster work. Note that if you wish to be available to comfort people with your therapy dog in the aftermath of a disaster you will need to do the necessary volunteer training to extablish your credentials. Contact the Red Cross or FEMA to find out what volunteer training is required to be approved for disasters. These criteria are constantly revised, so be sure to keep your credentials current.

Also contact your therapy dog registry and fulfill any training or testing requirements they may have. You need to have the necessary credentials for both yourself and your dog in advance or it is unlikely you will be allowed at the disaster site. While arrangements were speedily made for registered therapy dogs to serve after the Oklahoma City tragedy and the September 11th attacks, this is seldom feasible.

Disaster work can make emotional and physical demands on both handler and dog that may be beyond your ability to endure. A volunteer or a dog who is not up to it can do more harm than good. Sometimes the best way to help is to faithfully make your routine therapy dog visits to the people who need you and your dog more than ever at such a time.

## JOIN AN ESTABLISHED GROUP

The easiest way to start out as a therapy dog handler is usually to join a group. Joining a local group and a national group are both worthwhile. Each will have standards to determine whether or not you and your dog qualify, and guidelines for behavior on visits. Approval from a therapy dog group provides you with a helpful credential and a check on your own appraisal of your dog.

Your best choice of a national therapy dog registry to join with your dog depends on your locale. You'll usually get best support if you join the group most active in your area. If you wish to join a specific local group, you will need to register your therapy dog through the national group they use. Some local groups are independent of any national affiliation, and have strong standards as well as insurance. In such cases, this may serve as your only therapy dog registration.

Joining a group lets you find out if you enjoy this work and if you and your dog are suited for it. It lets you try therapy dog work without getting people in a facility attached to your dog before you're sure you want to make a commitment.

If after talking to a group's leader you feel you might be interested in joining, the first step is to attend a practice session. Don't bring your dog the first time, simply come to observe. Do you feel comfortable with the way they treat dogs? Would you and your dog be safe around these dogs? If so, talk to the leader about bringing your dog to a future session.

The next step is to attend a therapy dog visit with the group, without bringing your dog. This will give you a chance to observe the group in a facility. If you're unsure after this first visit, don't bring your dog as the next step. Instead, attend more visits as an observer, in different types of facilities.

If you feel uncomfortable around people with disabilities or in nursing homes or other facilities, this doesn't necessarily mean you wouldn't enjoy working there with a therapy dog. Most of us with empathy for other people feel uncomfortable in situations where people seem to be suffering.

Passing evaluation by a national therapy dog group is an excellent way to start your work, and safeguards against harm or disappointment to the people you and your dog will serve. On therapy dog visits, Star wore a harness with the patch insignia of the therapy dog registry, plus the registry's ID tag.

Three things will help you become comfortable on visits:
1. Give yourself three, four or more visits before making a decision. Like our dogs, we often get used to a situation with experience. Don't give up too soon.
2. Investigate possibilities for an orientation through a local nursing home or other facility similar to where you want to work. Facilities have programs to help volunteers cope with these common feelings.
3. Learn your job as a therapy dog handler. When you develop the needed skills to work your dog with people in the facility, you'll find your mind and  body focused on the good you accomplish with your dog. The atmosphere around you will become positive and happy. As you adjust to the situation, you'll often realize people aren't suffering as you thought they were. Excessive sympathy interferes with your ability to help people.

Besides the opportunity to try therapy dog work, starting with a group often means you work under someone capable of controlling a dog obedience class. This person can objectively evaluate you and your dog, give an opinion as to whether you're ready to do visits, and let you know how you're doing. He or she can often prevent problems from bringing a group of dogs together, mostly by well-timed reminders to handlers to watch their dogs.

If you have doubts about your dog's behavior, don't start therapy dog visits. Even if you think you and your dog are ready, it's wise to start with a skilled therapy dog instructor present.

## DEALING WITH OTHER DOGS

Working with a group tests your therapy dog's ability to work around other dogs. You will encounter other dogs in therapy dog work, even on one-dog visits. When a facility allows one therapy dog, it's likely to allow others, including such untrained dogs as the pets of family members visiting people who live in the facility. A dogfight presents one of the greatest risks of injury to people posed by the presence of dogs. The dogs seldom intend to bite people, but people get between the fighting dogs and are bitten.

Most therapy dogs are treasured. Not only do the owners love their dogs, but people in facilities become attached to them. Injury to a therapy dog hurts many people, and it takes a long time to select and train a new dog. Dogfights have ruined many a fine dog's attitude and behavior toward other dogs. The dog that "wins" can be just as damaged as the "loser," in terms of how each dog will behave around other dogs in the future.

This is one reason every therapy dog needs an attentive and skilled handler. A dog accustomed to your consistent attention will more readily leave it to you to deal with other dogs. If you neglect to watch and properly direct your dog, the dog may decide to take over the job of protecting itself and you from other dogs.

*Star's attention turned to her handler rather than to the other dog. This is the ideal response for a therapy dog when working. You condition this reaction by bringing your dog's attention back to you whenever it notices another dog on your outings.*

Therapy dog screening tests look carefully for the problem of aggression toward other dogs, and rightly so. If your dog passes the test, but you realize it is aggressive toward other dogs and you don't have complete control at all times, therapy dog visits are out of the question. No test is an absolute guarantee. Test results must always be balanced by everything else you know about your dog and about your handling skill.

Therapy dogs also encounter other species of animals in their work. I can remember encounters with cats, birds, a ferret, and horses on visits. I will not knowingly work a therapy dog around another animal that is not under control, but sometimes things happen. One handler had a monkey jump onto her dog's back. You must be able to control your dog, no matter what.

If you happen to have a dog who is terrified of cats, or uncontrollable around birds, that could keep the dog from being a therapy dog. But most situations of working your dog around other types of animals will be managed by teaching your dog to give attention to you when you say its name. See "Attention, Release," in chapter 5 for these instructions.

## STANDARDS AND UNINTERRUPTED SERVICE

A therapy dog group can help establish standards for therapy dog work in a community. The group will develop a good reputation if facilities experience consistent, problem-free visits from members.

Therapy dog groups are often affiliated with either obedience training organizations or animal welfare organizations. Some animal welfare organizations visit with trained dogs and handlers, while others require no training. I do not recommend that you take your dog on visits with untrained dogs or dogs straight from an animal shelter with no quarantine.

Animal welfare organizations are increasingly convinced of the value of training to solve dog problems and to make dogs more secure in their homes. They're understandably offended by harsh dog training. Since therapy dog training shouldn't be harsh and is exactly right for many animal shelter dogs, more and more animal welfare organizations are sponsoring training.

*Local therapy dog groups can coordinate with facility staff to provide consistent service. People get attached to the dogs, as this dear lady did to Angel. A replacement is important whenever a volunteer stops visiting, to prevent emotional harm to people.*

Another important service a group can provide is to make sure a facility has continuous therapy dog visits. If one handler quits, the group can send out another. Similarly, if there's a problem with a handler, the facility can contact the group leader and let the group deal with the problem. This puts experienced trainers and handlers on the job, instead of leaving facility staff to handle a situation without, perhaps, any real solution to offer.

## INSURANCE

Therapy dog handlers or groups who collect fees for therapy dog service require special, professional insurance. Volunteers, on the other hand, are less likely to be sued. For the volunteer therapy dog handler who does not accept money for visits, the national therapy dog registries provide insurance.

The risks in this activity are extremely low when trained dogs visit facilities with qualified volunteer owners. Most accidents occur when dogs live in facilities and work without handlers. Untrained dogs have also been involved in accidents, as have dogs handled by children without adequate adult supervision.

Belonging to a group gives some handlers a false sense of security. But you're just as responsible for your dog's behavior with a group as when working alone. Handlers need to carry proof of rabies vaccination and therapy dog registration on visits. In case of an accident, show every concern for the injured person and make sure medical treatment is provided. Follow the rules of reporting required by your therapy-dog insurance coverage. Your dog may be quarantined, at your expense, and would probably also be retired from therapy dog work.

When dogs are trained, screened by therapy dog registries, and constantly accompanied on visits by qualified handlers, injuries to humans are virtually nonexistent. The problems seem to arise when facilities decide to have dogs in without these important checks and balances. Humans tend to think of dogs as products. They think if they get a "good dog," they can toss it into a facility and let it be used as a toy, and all will be well.

But a dog, like a human, is a living, changing creature, constantly responding to its experiences: a process, not a product. The right handler is an essential part of the process of good therapy dog work. Expecting a dog to work without this partnership is unfair to the dog, and puts humans at risk of injury. Therapy dog testing rightly evaluates the handler and dog as a team.

## WORKING WITH FACILITY STAFF

Facility staff members can have difficulty locating volunteers for therapy dog visits. A therapy dog group probably won't have an office, although some affiliated with animal welfare or other organizations may. When there's no office, one person needs to take calls from facilities and schedule visits. It doesn't work well to change this job around among group members, because facilities won't be able to keep track of the changing phone numbers.

Local groups function in various ways. Some send out individual dogs and handlers. Others always send multiple dogs and handlers. The group leader usually coordinates with the facility to set up visits. If the leader isn't present at every visit, a member who is there will need to understand the group's way of working and be able to communicate with the staff.

Sometimes the staff will forget the dogs are coming. For a one-dog visit, this may not be a big problem, except for depriving the people of the benefit of anticipation. It's a greater problem when a group of handlers and dogs visits. The first qualified person to reach the facility needs to go in and let someone know the dogs are arriving. This person needs to be capable of explaining to the staff how to set up for the visit, in case the contact person in the facility is unexpectedly absent. Keep a businesslike, courteous, positive attitude. Staff people are used to dealing with volunteers, but they have to trust therapy dog handlers in a special way. They will be reluctant to let anyone who seems to have a personality problem bring a dog into the facility.

If you have trouble with a staff person, don't indulge your feelings. Others are probably having trouble with the person, too. The problem will usually get solved without your help, or

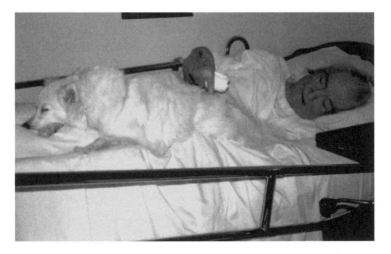

*Therapy dogs reach people through powerful communication without words.*

the staff person will find another job. Going to someone's superior often increases problems. When his or her superior says
you complained, the staff member may become much more negative toward you than before. You might have to take this risk if
the problem is serious.

Don't try to make a case for therapy dogs with negative staff
people by arguing. Just work your dog. You'll see an amazing
thing happen—the dog's nonverbal abilities and your good handling will reach them. Over time you'll see them respond to your
therapy dog, nonverbally at first. Eventually their words will
change, too. Sometimes the formerly hostile people become the
most enthusiastic!

Therapy dog work isn't done with words. Let the work
"speak" for itself. It's far more powerful than any words you
could use. Flawless behavior in the facility with your dog will
earn you the necessary time. Never force the dog on anyone.
Don't try to argue people out of their fears. The antidote to fear
is to replace it with love, and your therapy dog has what it takes.

## INDOOR OR OUTDOOR VISITS?

One important question about therapy dog visits is whether
to work indoors or outdoors at the facility. I visit indoors, except
for special events when everyone is outside. The weather in my
area wouldn't allow for consistent outdoor visits. Outdoor visits
can eliminate some of the people in the facility from participation, and put the dog at risk. If the facility wants you outdoors
because they lack trust in the dogs, you'll have to decide whether
to win their trust with good work outdoors, or suggest they call
back when they can arrange indoor therapy dog visits. Beware
of hot pavement, fleas, ticks, thorns, herbicides, pesticides, stray
dogs, and conditions too hot for a dog to work.

For a trained therapy dog, the ideal place for visits is indoors.
When the situation is looser, with dogs not groomed for the
indoors or with puppies, the session, not actually a therapy dog
visit, may belong outdoors.

## EDUCATION, ENTERTAINMENT OR THERAPY?

Each group needs goals for visits. This allows group members to function in harmony, and lets them clearly explain to facilities what they have to offer. Training clubs and other dog organizations may decide to concentrate on entertainment combined with petting at care facilities, and education combined with petting for schools and civic groups. The program for visits will depend on whether the group can practice together, on the training of the dogs, and on the priorities of the group.

When a group is unable to offer regular service to a facility, a brief presentation of obedience work and tricks will provide a stimulating social experience for people and reassure everyone the dogs are safe for petting. This introduces trained dogs to the community and gives new handlers an introduction to therapy dog work.

The ideal format for therapy dog work brings the same handler and dog or group back to each facility regularly. The staff learns what to expect, and people form bonds with the dog and handler. Performance is then unnecessary, although the dog needs to work under the handler's control at all times.

## COOPERATION AMONG GROUPS

Since many different kinds of groups make therapy dog visits, competitive friction can arise among groups. There are several reasons for groups to cooperate, and certainly enough work for everyone.

Facility staff learns about the benefits of therapy dog visits through professional organizations. They meet with each other locally and at national conferences, and they receive professional publications featuring therapy dog work. Universities and other organizations study the benefits of providing animals in health-care settings. This creates a growing demand for therapy dogs.

Many facilities have tried resident dogs unsuccessfully. They've tried puppies. They've tried untrained dogs and dogs handled by children. These programs sometimes work, but may cause safety concerns and staff complaints. A trained therapy dog brought to visit by a qualified volunteer handler meets the needs of almost all facilities.

When facilities learn what you have to offer, your services will be much in demand. This may take two or three years. Soon you'll have more requests for visits than you can fill, and will need to refer callers to other therapy dog handlers.

Another reason to refer a facility to another group is distance. Traveling long distances to visits may be necessary in rural communities, but in general the shorter the trip to and from the facility, the more energy handler and dog will have for the visit. Transportation costs are reduced, you can visit more consistently in marginal weather, and handlers feel stronger commitments to facilities in their own neighborhoods.

Cultivating good relations with other groups in your area can allow you to exchange volunteers. Sometimes a volunteer lives nearer another group or has preferences better suited to a different group's goals. If you have good communication and cooperation, you can refer these people to the best groups for them and conserve volunteers who would otherwise be lost entirely. Therapy dog groups in an area can also work together to help volunteers find training.

Courtesy among therapy dog groups is important if the public is to trust the concept of trained therapy dogs. Negative perceptions about therapy dogs arising from one group competitively criticizing another could make insurance a problem for all. This will not happen if people stick to the facts: insurance companies have nothing to fear from trained therapy dogs working with qualified handlers. Injuries are extremely rare.

## DOES THIS GROUP MAKE YOU PROUD?

The last consideration for a handler in deciding whether or not to join a particular group is whether you would be proud to belong to this group. That's a decision each handler has to make, and many factors apply. Do you share the group's goals? Are you satisfied with the competence of the other handlers?

*When deciding about joining a particular therapy dog group, consider: Would you be proud to belong to this group? Would your reputation and your dog be safe with this group? Are your goals for therapy dog work compatible with the group's goals?*

No one handler can do everything. The more you learn about the dizzying variety of dog activities available, the more choices you'll have to make. My choice, after originally starting with a local group, is to make therapy dog visits on my own with one nationally registered therapy dog at a time. I also enjoy working with one other handler and dog, when I can find the perfect partner match. Whatever you choose, you will benefit from group ties.

# 4

# VISITS WITH ONE DOG

Making therapy dog visits as an individual handler with one dog is a greater responsibility than working with a group. If you were to quit after having made enough visits for people to bond with the dog, you could cause emotional harm.

It also takes time for the staff to get used to you. Bringing a therapy dog program into a facility can be a complicated process. Someone may have worked hard to get all necessary permissions. If you quit, the facility faces starting over with a new volunteer. They may give up the idea entirely.

This would be a loss to other therapy dog volunteers, too, because generally handlers can't call facilities and be quickly accepted as volunteers. It's like applying for a job, since the facility will be at least partly responsible for your actions while you volunteer there. By causing a facility to become discouraged about working with therapy dog handlers, you could close the door to other volunteers looking for places to serve.

With the added responsibility of working as an individual handler also comes increased freedom. The dog is spared the constant pressure of other dogs, and the handler has more flexibility to work with people. My sessions are longer than when I worked with a group, but my dogs have consistently shown less fatigue.

*Taking responsibility for facility visits on your own requires an even more serious commitment than visiting with a group. Angel visited the same facilities for several years, and I have continued there with the other dogs. If your time commitment to therapy dog visits is occasional or seasonal, you will want to stay with a group.*

## WIN APPROVAL OF A GROUP

Because it's such a big responsibility to serve a facility on your own, it's usually best to stay in a group until you're sure you want to make a serious commitment to therapy dog work. If you decide to start making visits alone then, group ties will help. Groups receive requests from facilities for visits they can't fit into their schedules. Once the leader feels you're qualified, you can be given some of these referrals. Don't expect this to happen quickly. Reputation is important in therapy dog work.

Experience with a group will also screen your dog for working around other dogs. Even on one-dog visits, you will eventually encounter other dogs in facilities. But unlike group visits with other skilled dog trainers present, you may be the only one there who knows what can happen when two dogs meet, and how to prevent problems.

The other dog could be a resident pet, a family pet brought to visit, or a stray in the parking lot. The other dog may have no handler, or a handler who can't control the dog. Even in play, dogs can bump people and make them fall.

You and your dog must be at least as good around other dogs for one-dog visits as for visits with a group of other handlers and dogs.

If you are starting on your own because your area has no therapy dog group yet, or you are starting a group, there are good and bad ways to go about it. Too often, people start local therapy dog groups with no experience in the work and no trained dogs. A brochure, advertising and selling facilities on the idea of visits is not the place to start. Without the proper training, screening and experience for handlers and dogs, a group can quickly become known for complaints and broken promises. This is doubly sad when your group will be the first experience of therapy dog work for facilities in your area. The basic unit in therapy dog work is each skilled handler and dog. Make sure this unit is strong, and you can build the rest from there.

## WORKING WITH THE STAFF

When you work on your own, you take over the duties of scheduling visits and working closely with the staff. In the process, you learn more about how the facility benefits from your visits than when you have a group leader.

You also hear the negative things! Because volunteers are so important to facilities, staff will word any complaints tactfully. But complaints will come to you instead of going through the group leader. I like this chance to work problems out directly.

When a group of dogs visits a facility, the staff may not be able to provide a staff person to work with each handler and dog. But when you come on a visit with one dog, some facilities will have a staff person work with the people as you handle the dog. People derive maximum benefits from visits with strong staff support, and you get more feedback.

Many staff members don't understand therapy dog work. You may need to encourage them to participate. Tell them your preferences and how your dog works best. The staff can't give your visits the proper support unless you communicate with them. Experience on visits with a group will help you decide how you want to structure your therapy dog visits once you start going on your own.

A handler working alone can often schedule visits to eliminate difficulties unavoidable for a group. For example, I arrange visits when parking and traffic are light. Together with staff, I choose a time when the fewest competing activities are scheduled. I schedule nursing home visits when the most staff is available and and the people are most alert. I avoid weekends when families visit nursing homes with untrained dogs.

## QUIETER, LESS DISRUPTION TO FACILITY ROUTINE

Staff members appreciate how smoothly one-dog visits fit into the facility's routine. Many people in facilities cooperate better with staff for the rest of the day after the dog's visit. If you visit quietly in one or more central areas of the facility for an hour or so, staff can bring people out a few at a time, sometimes on the way to or from care. If you go to rooms, one dog causes less interference with facility routine than having several dogs and handlers visiting rooms in the facility at once. When staff in a facility is tight, one-dog visits divert less of this precious resource away from direct care for people.

*Visits with one dog can be quieter and less disruptive to the facility's routine. Angel, a nimble dog, stepped onto this sturdy, Formica-topped table to get closer to her friend.*

## STRONGER FOCUS

Providing a focal point for people such as those with Alzheimer's disease and children with learning disabilities works best when only one dog is in the room. When more than one dog is present, people's attention can flit from one dog to another. It can also take longer to deal with people's fear of dogs and get on to therapy.

## LIMITS

A major difference between group and individual visits is the number of people you can serve. You can perform in front of a large group with only one dog. If you want to let the people pet and interact with the dog, too large a group of people leaves many with nothing to do while you work the dog with a few at a time.

It's ideal for a person to have at least fifteen minutes with the dog if he or she shows strong interest. Just running quickly around the room for petting gives little opportunity for true therapy. Three or four people can sometimes share a fifteen-minute session, but some people will need the dog all to themselves.

A good guideline when you start is to limit visits to about an hour and the number of people the dog works with to about a dozen. You may need to limit a small dog to fewer people, and a large dog may comfortably work with more people. Experience will help you set more specific limits for your dog and for the facilities you visit.

Performance requires limits, too. On a group visit with other dogs and handlers, your dog might do some of the performance and rest during much of it. On a one-dog visit, your dog has to do the whole show. This cuts into its stamina for interaction with people.

Going from room to room is also tiring for the dog. To start, a limit of four rooms per therapy dog visit is a good guideline.

## ROOMS VERSUS MEETING AREAS

You'll need to decide with the staff where in the facility you and the dog will work. It will help to know some of the pluses and minuses about different ways of setting up the visit.

It's ideal if a staff person is available at all times on therapy dog visits. This is least expensive for nursing homes if you work in a central area or next to a nursing station. If they can't provide a staff member to work directly with you, at least in these locations you can hail one.

Why this criteria? One experience crystallized it for me. I was in a room with my miniature American Eskimo, Angel, when a disoriented woman clutched the little dog and began to squeeze, hard. The lady clearly wasn't going to let go, and was hurting Angel. The facility's social services director was with me. While I worked Angel as if she were having a veterinary procedure, keeping her attention focused on my voice and scratching behind her ears, the staff member gently pried the woman's hands loose. Angel wasn't injured or upset.

The handler must be able to control the dog, but handling people is up to the staff. Staff can tell you if a particular person might abuse the dog, and can step in and control people who might get rough. The handler's attention must be focused on the dog. I'm not saying you would be wrong to visit rooms without a staff person. It's something for you to decide.

In nursing homes, therapy dog handlers are often routed through the Social Services or Activities departments. The more consistent you are about your visits, the more the nursing staff will get involved. This means more benefits to people, because nurses and other caretakers work more closely with people and know their specific therapeutic needs.

You can stick to room visits and not work in common areas at all, though you will probably find yourself stopped on the way to and from the rooms you visit to work with others who want to see the dog. You may develop relationships with certain people and go straight to their rooms. After you know them, having a staff person there may become unimportant.

*Meeting areas offer social benefits, such as Star's participation in the adult day facility's rhythm band. Room-to-room visits reach people who can't come out to join the group. Handlers who choose either type of visit provide benefits for people.*

Consider the dog's preferences, too. My therapy dog Star seemed most comfortable in settings with limited traffic through the room. She preferred meeting with people in one area rather than going from room to room through the facility. She needed about five minutes to settle into each new location, so was more relaxed if the day's visit took place in only one area.

Star made room-to-room visits when she was young, and later in life in the cooler times of year. During summers and for the last year of her career, I arranged to make those visits with one of my other therapy dogs instead. My other therapy dogs have all enjoyed "exploring" from room to room. Be sure to consider your dog's needs in every situation.

## MAKING CHANGES

The way you prefer to work will change as you learn, and as you work with different dogs. Staff members change what they want from you, too, and staff people leave their jobs and are replaced. All these are opportunities to change your routine.

One of the hardest changes for me was from performances to quiet interactions with people. My dogs have been good performers. Staff formed the habit of bringing everyone out for a show and coming back to get them when the show was over. If you start your work in a facility by performing, it can be difficult to change the routine. The staff may not realize interaction with the dog is more therapeutic for people, especially if staff members stay busy doing other things when you're there and don't get involved in therapy dog visits. Once I even found myself in a recreation room too cold for the people, and no staff to take them back to their rooms. I finally recruited someone from the administrative office to come to the rescue.

Another problem comes when, in order to get people out of their rooms, the staff has told them the dog is going to do tricks. If you have one dog and the staff has assembled thirty people, how can you include them all except by doing a performance?

If you decide to eliminate performance work the facility has grown to expect from you, you'll need the staff's help. They can stop bringing a large group out at once, and start telling people you and your dog are coming to visit, not for tricks. At one facility I visit, it had been the custom for the desk person, seeing a dog arrive, to announce a dog show over the public address system. We had to get him to stop making the announcement when he saw Angel.

An adult day-care facility I used to visit filled the day with activities to stimulate people, a primary function of the program. At 10:30 a.m., they needed short, snappy presentations for the whole group at once, allowing for little interaction between participants and the dog. I inquired about changing our time to early morning, when the facility opened. I began coming with the dog at 7:30 a.m., and visiting quietly with people as they arrived. When they started the first program in midmorning, the dog and I would leave. The change worked well.

## THE APPROACH

One-dog visits give you great responsibility as well as great flexibility in how you approach people with your dog. Particularly in

*Star loved shaking hands with people, and offered her paw gently. After the initial approach, having the dog shake hands is one way to stimulate interaction between the person and the dog.*

nursing homes, handlers encounter people who, when asked if they would like to pet the dog, immediately say no. Sometimes it's the first choice people have had all day, and they reject the dog just to feel some control over their lives. Unfortunately, this not only makes the handler feel rejected, but also deprives the person being visited of benefits from the dog.

People will also say no because they misunderstand or don't hear the question, because they don't want to monopolize the dog, or because they feel self-conscious in the center of group attention. As handlers we can often turn these "no" answers into "yes" answers, but we must respect people's wishes, and our time is limited. You might want to try my tactic. I seldom ask, "Would you like to pet the dog." Instead I read people's body language and occasionally ask "Do you like dogs?" I bring the dog near those people who seem attracted to it. I also take cues from the staff.

To encourage petting, I pet the dog myself and say, "He (or she) likes to be petted." If two or three people are with the dog, I let them know the dog enjoys being petted by more than one person at once. My dogs will often turn their backs for petting. I let people know the dog wants a back rub, so they won't think the dog doesn't like them! The dog's back or the back of its head are sometimes better to offer for petting, especially to nervous people.

For a person seated in a wheelchair, I may start by placing the dog side-by-side with the chair, facing the same direction as the person. The person can pet the dog's head and talk to the dog, and the dog can turn its head to the person without the person feeling confronted by the dog's teeth. Many people want the dog to walk right up and slip its furry head under an out-stretched hand, so that's what I direct the dog to do in those cases.

I alter these positions whenever necessary to make it possible for the person to reach the dog. Seating the dog in a chair has worked well for Star and Gabriel, both agile Belgian Tervuren. I typically cue the dog to jump into the chair, and to turn the way I indicate with a hand gesture, facing toward or away from the person depending on the person's wishes. I lift the dog down from the chair, to spare its joints.

In one facility where the visiting room was small, the staff would pack the wheelchairs tight around Star, with the footrests converging in front of her chair. To remove her safely without risk of scratching anyone's feet, I would sometimes have to lift her out over the back of her chair! She weighed fifty pounds and liked being lifted, which turned out to be a good thing later in her career, when, on two occasions, psychiatric patients suddenly picked her up in their arms. You never know what might happen on a therapy dog visit!

Your personality will determine your approach to people. I prefer to approach quietly and avoid triggering rejection. No matter how objective we try to be, having people turn us away will register at some level in our feelings. Other handlers may enjoy risking rejection with a more overt and exciting approach, which can be stimulating and is the best method with some people. When you work with the staff, they may make the approach instead of you, which lets you experience different styles. As long as you are courteous and respect everyone's feelings, the best approach is the one you find most comfortable.

With experience, you will probably build a repertoire of ways to approach different types of people. This comes with time. Let your individual style develop naturally, paced to keep you confident of control over the dog. Be prepared for the person who at first rejects the dog to do an about-face and want to join the petting, especially after seeing others pet the dog.

## WORKING WITH CHILDREN

I used to serve a day care for children with disabilities, where performance helped the children develop mental and social skills and form an understanding of working dogs. These demonstrations for the children were brief, but I saw four or five groups in a morning, a lot of demonstrating! I found ways to relieve stress on the dog. One was to have the dog stationed in one room, away from classrooms. Working in "its own" room, the dog settles in and is spared the stress of adjusting to a new environment for each group.

If the dog gets hot or thirsty, I stop at any time during a visit or presentation to offer water (people love to see the dog receive this care), but the break between groups in this program was another chance for the dog to drink. If a group had pushed the dog too hard, the break let me give some tennis balls to catch, or some other diversion to forget the negative experience.

*Saint adored children. When children are under age 7, it's best to have no more than 4 children actually interacting with the dog at one time. Children develop empathy around 5 to 7 years of age, and larger groups become feasible.*

Working the dog away from classrooms can benefit the children and the school. A child severely afraid of dogs or allergic to them can remain in the classroom with supervision while others come to see the dog. If the dog were to visit the classroom, the allergic child would be exposed not only during the visit, but also after the dog left, since allergens would linger.

If the school unknowingly brings an allergic child to the dog in a room away from the regular classroom, the exposure is limited to the time of the visit. The child goes back to the classroom in a few minutes, and any allergic reaction is sure to be lessened. Childhood allergies can be life threatening, so please do not overlook this risk.

Children whose behavior makes it unsafe for them to be around the dog can also remain in the classroom. The teachers know which children might get out of control. Having the visit outside the classroom gives teachers this important option.

Fearful children should not be pressured at all. If they don't come into the session with the dog, they'll still hear about it from classmates. Over time, they'll develop a desire to come see the dog. If they still don't like the dog near them, keep a distance. Let them watch for as many visits as they wish. What they'll see is a dog always under a handler's control, interacting with their happy classmates. They will nearly always overcome their fear eventually, and want to pet the dog. This is how it needs to happen, not by pushing them to accept the dog in one session.

Some young children go through a developmental fear period about dogs, not caused by any bad experiences with dogs. If they have good dog experiences and no bad ones, they outgrow it. As with any other fear, it is essential for handler and staff to avoid pushing the child into contact with the dog.

## FIRST VISITS AWKWARD

Expect your first three or four visits to any facility to be awkward. The staff doesn't know how to work with you yet, the people may be uncertain about the dog, bonds take time to form and you may not know at first exactly how you want to work there. Things get a lot smoother after the first few visits, and continue to get better and better. Many volunteers quit in the first months. Staff members will work with you more and people will respond more strongly to the dog when they realize you're going to keep coming.

Most studies of therapy dog work have been based on short-term study projects rather than consistent, long-range programs. I see increased improvements at one year, at two years—it never seems to stop growing. The longer you continue your visits, the more the people respond, and you and the dog enjoy the work more, too.

## FACILITY CHOICES

Volunteer where you will be happy and will have a happy, comfortable dog. Some facility therapy dog programs attract large numbers of handlers, often more than their fair share of the available local volunteers. Restrictive rules help them screen and manage volunteers who may be serving in their first therapy dog assignments. Sometimes the people running the programs are not particularly knowledgeable about dogs.

If the rules conflict with the best care for your dog or with your happiness as a volunteer, you have two good choices. You can discuss your concerns about the rules with those in charge to see if rules can be changed or a formal exception made for you. Or you can choose to "vote with your feet," and seek out a different facility to serve instead of that one.

One choice not appropriate for a responsible volunteer is to agree to a rule, then consistently violate it. For example, if your dog were always clean, perhaps "no one would ever know" about your bathing schedule. The problem is, going along with an inappropriate rule helps the rule become even more deeply entrenched, and at the same time skews opinions and research results being formulated about therapy dog work.

Change can be scary. As you gain experience, you may find yourself increasingly restless with a particular program you serve. If others are eager to join the program with their dogs, your changing to a setting more compatible with your personality and your dog's needs won't leave anyone without therapy dog service. Talk to local therapy dog group leaders and see if any other facilities have requested service. It may be awkward at first to go on your own, but within a few visits you're likely to find deep satisfaction.

When you first visit a new facility, suggest to them a "try-out," not committing to a regular program until you can tell if you and your dog will be happy. Take it easy at first, expressing to facility staff your dog's needs, while listening and learning about theirs.

Please don't let a misfit between you and a particular facility cause you to drop out of therapy dog work. Good volunteers will always be needed. You may have to poke your nose around your community to find the perfect spot, but your search will be bountifully rewarded.

## THE LEASH

You may find you'll work your dog off leash more on one-dog visits than on group visits, but this must be a moment-by-moment decision. A handler has to constantly assess risks. The

*A high degree of training and a powerful rapport between attentive handler and therapy dog are necessary before you consider removing the leash. Angel worked from the top of her platform on a reliable stay command. A leash dangling from the platform would have been a hazard.*

leash should be on unless the dog is working on command and the leash needs to be off for some reason. The dog should never be off leash unless the dog is just as reliable off leash as on leash. Most dogs and handlers never have this much control.

A handler on a one-dog visit might feel a false sense of security with no other dogs there. But what if another dog unexpectedly arrives? Consider also whether you have enough off-leash control over your dog to keep it from bumping or tripping a fragile person, or a staff member rushing to an emergency? Are you sufficiently familiar with the facility routine and traffic patterns to see someone coming and move your loose dog in time? Are you prepared for absolutely anything, in handling your dog at any given moment?

Whenever a therapy dog on a visit with its handler isn't wearing a physical leash, there must be a flawless "mental leash" between dog and handler. Unless you are absolutely sure of this level of training and focus with your dog, never remove the leash. Needless to say, the leash must also be on whenever the rules require it.

# THERAPY DOGS

# 5

# CONDITIONING THE DOG TO HANDLING

A therapy dog must have plenty of hands-on touch, in training and throughout its working life. Your time spent conditioning the dog to touch and to other motivators becomes a tremendous asset when teaching a therapy dog anything, including commands. Touch is integral to the training of a therapy dog because therapy dogs must be comfortable with touch at any point during their work. As your dog learns to respond to handling, you develop the necessary skills and knowledge, too.

## MOTIVATORS: FOOD, PRAISE, PETTING, AND PLAY

You have four main tools to motivate your dog to do as you ask. The first is food. Food is popular among professional trainers as well as pet owners. It's helpful for teaching young puppies and for directing a dog's attention without using force. It can help you get a dog to try something new or overcome a fear, including a new dog's fear of you. A therapy dog's training is not complete, though, until it can work without food treats.

The second motivator is praise. Praise can't be overused, with two exceptions. Praising a dog for expressing dangerous instincts such as aggression toward people or animals makes the instincts stronger, a problem for dogs with instincts best kept dormant. Second, avoid praising a dog when it acts afraid, because you might then make the dog think its fears are valid.

*Daily grooming is perhaps the most valuable use of your time with a therapy dog. In a few minutes, the dog receives control work practice, cuddling with you, a brief physical exam, skin care, coat maintenance, and handling to help it stay tolerant of all kinds of touch. This is conditioning to handling at its best.*

Pure praise uses voice and body language, without touch. Your most effective voice for praise varies from one dog to another. As you talk to your dog and note its reactions, you can fine-tune your praise. You'll also learn how to use your voice to tell the dog you're displeased, to give a verbal command, to encourage the dog to keep working, and as a lifeline to hold your dog steady under stress.

Dogs learn body language more easily than they learn words, and a good handler notices and controls his or her movements. Since your dog will be aware of every detail, you can convey messages by combining your body language with verbal language. You can also develop body language communication for situations where your dog can't hear you, or where you don't wish to use words.

Sensitivity to both verbal and body language should be cultivated to the highest degree in a therapy dog. This requires spending as much time as possible with your dog. Keeping the dog in the house with you is a great help.

The more effort you make to respond to a dog's communication, the more the dog will work to respond to yours. Many owners who think their dogs are stupid have not given them enough attention or encouragement to communicate. Children show the same mental dullness when given as little stimulation as many dogs are given. Attentive, caring owners tend to create bright, responsive dogs.

Equally important when working with the therapy dog is the third motivator, petting, or touch. It's not instinctive for a dog to enjoy being touched. A dog's normal reaction is defensive, un-

*Petting is a major motivator for training. Building your dog's enjoyment of petting to the highest possible level will greatly benefit therapy dog work, and is a primary goal of conditioning the dog to handling.*

less it has learned in a deep, emotional way to trust. This response must be conditioned through consistently pleasant touch. It is the handler's responsibility to keep up this conditioning throughout a therapy dog's career.

A therapy dog will be petted a great deal by gentle, considerate people. People will also touch the dog inappropriately at times. The handler compensates for inappropriate touch with good touch, to keep the dog tolerant. Pleasant touches should always outnumber unpleasant touches by at least ten to one.

Look at the circumstances surrounding the touches, too. For example, if a man mistreats or frightens the dog, you then need to arrange a large number of pleasant experiences with men to prevent the dog from deciding all men are bad. Better yet, don't let it happen in the first place.

Petting can become a strong motivator for your dog. I used to let Saint go back to the tracklayer (who, after walking the track, follows handler and dog in case they need guidance) for petting, as a reward at the end of a successful scent track. Petting by someone he didn't see every day was a reward for Saint. Building in a therapy dog a deep enjoyment of being petted by you and by others will be a great asset in your work.

A puppy deprived of human contact may never be fully at ease with people. Puppyhood, up to about 11 weeks of age, is a critical period for socialization. An unsocialized dog can sometimes be reclaimed, but it's a long process. There is some evidence the chief means of making up this lost time is through play, which is the fourth motivator for working your dog.

Like people, dogs use play to learn and to form relationships. Not all dogs play easily with humans. Some are not playful by nature, and others never learn because their owners don't know how to play with them. The more games you teach your dog, the more tools you'll have for communicating, training, conditioning to handling, and exercise. We'll talk more about play later in this chapter.

*Bill and Star demonstrate the foundation of the Down-Stay command. The dog learns to remain in the Down position as the handler sits alongside and continually helps the dog. This preparation greatly reduces fear or confusion for the dog in more advanced stay training.*

## TEACHING THE DOG TO REMAIN STILL

One of the first things you can teach your dog through conditioning to handling is to remain still. This comes before any training to Stay on command. The dog with the most trouble being still, trying to squirm free when held, perhaps banging its head back and forth and kicking with all four legs when held on its back, is the dog who needs this handling most.

Conditioning your dog to remain still will aid in visits to the veterinarian and in emergencies. The Stay command is basic to all dog training. Without it, you can't teach a dog much of anything.

I've had some dramatic experiences when the dog's relaxation to my touch saved the day. One such experience was when young Saint tried to jump over a wire crate and got caught, screaming and hanging from one alarmingly bent leg. I was able to lift him clear and carry him to the bed to calm down and let me check him. Within a minute or two, he declared himself uninjured.

Another crisis came when Saint, playing the silly game of leading Star around by her wide nylon buckle collar, got his tooth stuck. She thought he was refusing to let her go, and panicked.

The ground was slick with ice, and it took me a few minutes to get to them. Star was growling and trying frantically to run, yanking Saint around, and I had to feel for the problem in the dark with my hands. It was awesome to feel both dogs instantly relax at my touch. I freed Saint quickly, and the relieved dogs soon seemed to forget all about it. We solved the collar problem by changing Star to a narrow nylon collar for her tags.

These dogs didn't settle to my touch just because they loved me. Your dog can love you with all its heart and still react badly to your touch. They didn't respond because I had obedience trained them, either. Dogs can be obedience trained with virtually no conditioning to positive touch.

Saint and Star relaxed instantly because of years of connecting my touch with love and safety. You can achieve the same thing with your dog by putting in the time and handling your dog with consistently positive touch. In the process, you will dramatically add to your dog's safety in therapy dog work.

Some dogs can't be rewarded with petting in obedience class because they get overexcited. This problem results from owners not spending enough time petting their dogs. Of course, this would be a terrible problem in therapy dog work.

If you condition your dog properly, it will come to you, look to you, listen to you and respond to your touch in a true emergency. If you induce panic deliberately in your dog, especially repeatedly, the dog will learn to avoid you in times of stress. Don't try to trick your dog into thinking someone else caused the pain or fear. Don't try to fool your dog into thinking something you set up was an accident. Don't use terrorist tactics in dog training. In order to be a successful therapy dog, your dog needs to trust you, and to trust friendly strangers and the working situation.

When conditioning the dog to remain still, start with continuous touch. Whatever contact induces your dog to stop moving is good: scratch the inside of the thigh (my husband discovered the magic of this with Saint), rub the tummy or chest, scratch behind the ears, encircle the dog with your arms or hold it in your lap. If the dog panics when you hold it still, find what your dog can easily tolerate well short of panic and work up slowly from there. This reaction would be an indication of a dog not suited for therapy dog work.

You can lie down or sit alongside the dog. For a small enough dog, you can rest it on your legs on its back, faced toward you and then away from you. The more variations, the better. A therapy dog can work with humans at all kinds of physical angles, but only if the dog learns it first with you.

Whatever the position, stroke the dog and talk in a pleasant voice as you hold it. Some dogs relax into this fairly naturally. It's a desirable trait to look for when testing a new dog, and to teach to the dog you have.

Allow the dog to stir lightly to ask you to release it, but don't release immediately. Get it to settle again first, then release. You want your dog to be able to ask, then to accept your decision. If you release instantly when the dog struggles, you're giving up control. Even worse is to hold on as the dog struggles more and more, and then finally let go. This teaches a dog to persist and escalate in struggling against you.

Be in a position to win. You want the dog to learn patience and trust in you. You need this control for real-life situations, as well as for the right relationship with your dog.

You don't want to squelch your dog's willingness to communicate with you, so if there's no reason to keep the dog still, release it shortly after it asks and settles again. Reward correct behavior by giving the dog what it wants, which in this case is to get free. Have yourself and your dog in comfortable positions whenever you work on this skill. Make it pleasant for the dog, and for yourself.

## PICKING UP THE DOG

Whether your dog is small or large, you would do well to learn (if you're strong enough) to pick the dog up whenever you wish. This improves your relationship with your dog, and gives you more options in unusual situations.

Here Angel participates when lifted, starting with putting her paws up on Bill's forearm as he reaches down to support her rear. Notice he is supporting her front legs between her "wrists" and her elbows. This is much safer for the dog than holding her by the paws.

Secure, comfortable and happy when held, Angel was able to interact with people on therapy dog visits from this position when needed.

A dog of any size who is being held up in the air needs to be fully supported to feel secure.

Picking up a dog of any size is not necessarily an easy skill. Many people lift even toy-sized dogs improperly. Always use both hands, no matter how small the dog. Improper lifting can cause the dog pain, or you may drop the dog and cause a terrible injury. Putting the dog back down is equally delicate, since leaping out of your arms can cause injury. Gabriel and I practiced me lifting him and then setting him back down many times before we mastered this skill as a team. He had to learn to calmly let me set him back down, and I had to learn his body structure. Most of this practice took place while I was watching television and he was soliciting someone to throw his tennis ball! Believer has gone through the same training process.

You need not train the therapy dog to be picked up by just anyone; in fact, I recommend not allowing the staff or other people in facilities to pick up your dog. It's too easy for the dog, not knowing someone else's moves, to zig when it should zag, and get hurt. This not only risks injury, but it can also ruin the dog's trust.

If it's too late to stop someone from picking up your dog by the time you notice, don't grab or yell. Watch carefully, and be ready in a split second to distract the dog if the person starts to hurt it. Next time, be more careful.

How should you pick up your dog? Have your veterinarian show you, if you aren't absolutely sure. In general, hold the dog against your body using both hands. The dog will learn to help you by tensing the right muscles as you lift. If your dog is too large or heavy for you to securely lift, you will want to focus instead on how to assist in such situations as safely getting it into position for interaction with someone who can't reach the dog on the floor. Use your veterinarian as a resource to make sure all maneuvers are safe.

## GAMES TO PLAY... WORK THAT TAIL!

Okay, your dog enjoys petting, holds still as you maintain physical contact and lets you pick it up, if you're strong enough. Now you can use games to teach more about touch.

Since therapy dogs interact with people, and since play is a major way dogs interact, teaching therapy dogs to play with humans is important. Some dogs are not playful, or only play games unsuited for therapeutic interaction. It's still well worth the time to play these games with your dog at home, because they strengthen your relationship, and aid both conditioning to handling and training for control. Play can be used to build in your dog the drives to work, to follow through on a task and to please you.

As you progress in training, you will use play to help your dog learn to obey a command when it isn't in an alert, ready-to-work mode. This is an essential control skill for a therapy dog, because often the dog will be interacting with someone else when you give a command. Start by playing games at home and inserting them between control exercises, when no one else is around to be inconvenienced or endangered if the dog is slow to come back to work.

Gradually you can develop in your dog the ability to play when you want to play, to work when you want to work and to shift gears from one to the other smoothly, at your wish. But don't expect this at the beginning. If you do, you'll dampen the dog's enjoyment of play, and damage one of your strongest motivators for training.

What games can you play with your dog? The rest of this chapter will give you ideas, and you and your dog will develop many of your own. Keep in mind the behavior you wish to encourage in your dog, and the behavior you wish to discourage. Maintain the ability to stop the game at any point.

Often the best correction for a dog getting too rowdy in play is for you to simply refuse to play anymore. It's not a dominant act, and therefore will work with an untrained puppy or a dog with which you don't yet have a solid relationship. This negative feedback teaches the dog to play more appropriately in future.

Stop the game for at least fifteen minutes, long enough to calm an overstimulated dog. If you restart the game and the dog again misbehaves, stop immediately. On the second or third repetition, the dog begins to understand what's wrong. Repetition is an important learning tool. Also, stop the game whenever the dog's teeth touch you in play. Don't let the dog think it's okay to put teeth on people.

With all games, play with your dog when you feel like it. Don't give the dog control of when you play, or for how long. You can allow your dog to solicit play, and you can play if you want to in response to the dog's request. This helps the dog learn to communicate with you. But if you're not in the mood, refuse.

Most dog trainers prefer to work with dogs that desire to please humans. This is an extremely helpful trait in a therapy dog. Some dogs simply haven't been conditioned properly to develop this trait. Play can help, offering many ways to enhance your dog's intelligence and ability.

As you play with your dog, take a good look at the tail. Become an expert on your dog's tail. In therapy dog work, the tail tells many tales! When Saint worked with young children, I noticed sometimes he insisted on standing when I asked him to sit. Finally I realized he knew something I didn't know. When he sat, three-year-old children were more likely to step on his tail. A smart dog taught me a new criteria for working with children.

Children showed me something else about the tail. One of his best friends in the day care program for children with disabilities was blind, and she loved to feel his high tail gently brush her face when she stood next to him to pet him. Other children sometimes brushed their own faces with his tail. Since a dog's tail is on the floor when it sits, this is not a tactile experience you would particularly want to encourage in people. It certainly points out the need to include the tail in grooming, and to thoroughly and frequently handle your dog's tail yourself. Include occasional playful pulling, to make sure the dog will not overreact to the sensation.

Notice, too, where your dog's tail rests when the dog sits. If a dog normally carries its tail low, it may sit on the tail, which is nice in therapy dog work, leaving no tail for anyone to crunch underfoot or roll over with a wheelchair. You can condition some dogs to sit this way, but be gentle about it, so the training doesn't create any problems. Always take responsibility for guarding the dog's tail when working around people. If the dog's position leaves the tail too vulnerable, I tuck it under the seated dog's leg, shift the dog's position to get the tail out of the flow of traffic, or stand over the tail myself to protect it.

Some types of tails present a real problem in therapy dog work, and require the handler's constant vigilance. When a dog holds the tail straight out, and especially if it tends to vigorously wag, the picture may be charming, but the sensation can be stinging! The handler now has to monitor six sides of the dog: what's going on at the dog's face, where each foot is (not putting weight on anyone) and what is in the path of the exuberant tail. So, take the tell-tale tail into consideration in your choice of a therapy dog, condition the tail to handling, and keep it in mind at all times when you work the dog in public.

## ATTENTION, RELEASE

You need to be able to get your therapy dog's attention instantly, without having to depend on the leash. With a puppy or new dog, start this process with food. As you establish strong play interaction with your dog, it's easy to change to a play reward. Throughout the process you want to build your praise and petting in the dog's mind as powerful reinforcers. The method here, which I learned from expert trainer Linda Newsome, will give you enormous ability to get your dog's attention whenever you need it.

To use food for attention training, conceal the food on your body. You don't want the dog to see the food until after it has heard the praise and you are ready to immediately give the food reward. Use small treats, easily gulped. Carry and give the food in such a way as to direct the dog's eyes to your eyes. When you have the dog's eyes, the rest follows. Give the food from your fingertips, held in the line between the dog's eyes and yours.

Say your dog's name, step backwards, praise the dog as it comes with you, then whip out a treat and give it. Repeat the sequence three to five times, so the dog won't learn to grab one treat and then turn attention away from you again.

Sustain the dog's attention and your eyes on the dog's eyes until you release with a Release word such as "Okay." I also use a signal with the Release, casting both arms outward. I encourage the dog to run to me for petting on the release. If I want to let the dog go play, I say "Okay, Go!" with the signal.

Repeat this exercise occasionally, in all possible locations, until you can get your dog's attention anytime, anywhere. If your dog cannot pay attention to you in a particular setting, the two of you need more training before starting therapy dog visits.

As your dog matures and develops an eager response to your petting and praise, you will not need to carry food any longer. By not showing the food until time to give it to the dog, you will build your dog's response to praise, and prevent food from becoming either a "bribe," or part of the actual command in the dog's mind. If the dog always sees food when you give a command, it's understandable if the dog doesn't think you are giving a command unless you show food! If the dog loves a particular toy, carrying the toy to drop to the dog's mouth after the praise can help make the transition. My favorite toy for this is a tennis ball through which I have drawn a length of braided nylon rope. I have some with short ropes, great for tossing when you don't want the ball to bounce or roll very far. I also have some balls with rope a couple of feet long, which allow the dog to catch the ball without my releasing the rope.

Always use movement, having the dog move with you, as a part of the attention work. Then the dog will understand you have a reason when you ask for attention. If you condition your dog to attention early, the later training and therapy dog handling will be easier. You will also be able to use attention to control your dog's perceptions of people, places and things you encounter together during your social skills training.

On therapy dog visits, people will constantly ask your dog's name. If you want a therapy dog to also participate in competition work, you may decide to have a completely separate name for the high-drive competition arena. Otherwise, saying the name over and over when you really do not need the dog's full attention will damage the response.

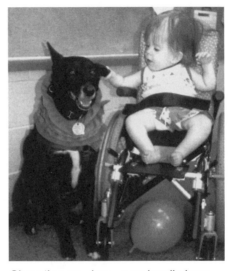

If your dog is not involved in competition work, be observant about your ability to get your dog's attention whenever you need it. Your tone of voice may cue your therapy dog as to whether you need full attention or are just telling someone the name. Due to this social aspect of the job, it is often appropriate to repeat a

*Since therapy dogs occasionally have people handle their ears unexpectedly, ear pinch in training for the retrieve could create problems. The dog needs to perceive all touch as positive, and believe any painful touch was an accident.*

command for a therapy dog when you would not repeat it with a competition dog.

## RETRIEVING

Retrieving is the healthiest and most popular game people play with dogs. It's best to teach retrieving in play before you start formal work to make it a command. The first rule is to never punish your dog when you take anything out of its mouth or when it brings something to you.

*Training for the Hold It begins by gently placing the dumbbell into the dog's mouth as you say "Take It." Star loved her dumbbell, and here is seen reaching for it as most dogs will begin doing when they've learned to associate it with good times.*

*Support the dog's chin while it holds the dumbbell. This helps the dog gently learn what "Hold It" means.*

When your dog has something in its mouth you don't want it to have, give it something nice in return for giving you the object. For this purpose I keep lots of dog toys around, and make the replacement toy exciting by playing with the dog for a moment before letting the dog have the toy all to itself. This teaches the dog to give up things without resentment or a sense of loss. I also have the dog give me whatever it has in its mouth so I can see if the object is safe for the dog to have. If the object isn't a problem, I give it back to the dog.

When your dog brings something to you or you have to take something out of its mouth, don't pull on the object. This en-

Say "Give" to command the dog to release the dumbbell to your hand.

The dog discovers it can walk and hold the dumbbell at the same time!

courages the dog to bite harder and resist you. Some dogs will easily give up the object if you just place your hand on it with no pressure. Another tactic is to grasp the dog's upper jaw by slipping your fingers behind one or both canine teeth, firmly but gently. With your other hand, remove the object from the dog's mouth. Don't let it be a fight between you and the dog. Just take control.

The handler who wishes to train a therapy dog to retrieve reliably on command for competition or hunting should shop carefully for the best method. For therapy dog and companionship purposes, it requires no force to develop an adequate retrieve in a dog born with strong retrieving instincts. If, when you throw an object, your dog runs out, picks it up and carries it, whether to you or off to play, it's promising. If your dog lacks

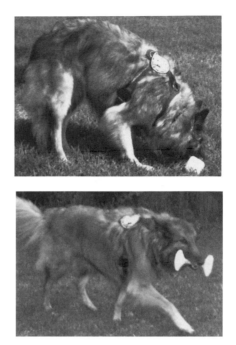

*The play retrieving drive you have built in your dog combines with the training, so that your dog will run out, pick up the dumbbell and carry it back to you. If at any time your dog fails to retrieve, you can run excitedly to the object with the dog, slip it gently into the dog's mouth, support the mouth back to the starting point, and praise the dog.*

this degree of instinct, you need not teach a therapy dog to retrieve at all. Or you can choose a structured method such as the one in the book *Dog Training for Dummies*, by Jack and Wendy Volhard, which is perfectly appropriate for a therapy dog.

For the dog who possesses natural retrieving instinct, Take It and Hold It can be taught as gentle, stationary exercises, after the dog has begun retrieving in play (brings the object back to you after you throw it, most of the time). Use a standard wooden or plastic dumbbell. Make sure the dog can comfortably hold it by the bar, without getting poked in the eye.

Don't force the Take It. Just gently place the dumbbell into the dog's mouth. The ability to confidently handle the dog's mouth is important for a therapy dog handler. If necessary, open the mouth by grasping the upper jaw, without causing the dog to bite its lips or tongue. With the object in the dog's mouth, say, "Hold it," and support the dog's chin, so the dog won't drop the chin and then the object.

After the dog gets used to this, start taking your supporting hand away. Before putting the dumbbell in, offer it to the dog, saying, "Take it." Any time the dog takes the dumbbell without your help, give liberal praise; this is an excellent sign. Build time on the Hold It gradually, counting the seconds. Decide in advance: it will be five seconds this time, or thirty seconds, or one minute, and help the dog finish the time before you release. Don't just release when you see the dog about to quit.

If the dog drops the dumbbell while on the Hold It command, go back to holding the dog's mouth. This is a slow process, but it will work, without doing any harm to your dog's working ability or attitude toward you.

When you take the dumbbell out of the dog's mouth, use the word you want for your command to release the object. Some say "Out," others say "Give." I occasionally say "Thank you!" This command can also be used when you take a forbidden object from your dog around the house.

Once the dog holds the dumbbell reliably when seated, put the leash on and begin having the dog stand up and walk with it. The dog may get a panicky look in its eyes and have trouble at this point; it will not believe it can hold the dumbbell and walk at the same time. Patiently help the dog through this period, supporting the jaw again, and it will progress quickly. Gradually walk the dog on leash farther with the dumbbell in its mouth. Then start leaving the dog on Hold It in a Stay, and call the dog to you.

When the dog is steady, you can put your retrieve together, combining play with command control. The whole retrieving process takes a mature dog quite awhile, but for a dog like Gabriel who already loved to retrieve in play, teaching Hold It took only two weeks, started after he had been with me a few months. I started it with Believer at age seven months when she came to me, and it took longer but the results were more gratifying. She started out unwilling to retrieve at all, and five months later is eager as can be!

Extended retrieving games, in which you hide something from the dog and the dog seeks it out, let you observe your dog's working style and encourage persistence when working at a task. Make the game a little challenging, but not hard enough to discourage the dog. It's fine to use food as the object, especially at first. At my house, the Easter cookie hunt, where all my dogs run through the yard finding dog biscuits dropped along my footsteps, is a delightful dog tradition.

## SAFETY HINTS FOR RETRIEVING DURING VISITS

1. Give retrieving commands only when the dog has room to move. Avoid these games in unfenced areas.

2. Keep the leash on for retrieving games in which others throw the object for the dog. Make sure the dog has a clear path to the ball before you release. Use the leash to stop the dog from running into people or snapping teeth at the ball near them. This requires considerable handling experience and skill with the leash. I do not recommend a retracting leash for this situation.

3. When a group is taking turns throwing the ball, have the dog bring you the object for you to pass to the next person. The dog would not understand to take it to the next person or not to, in the case of an unruly child who needs to miss a turn. This also prevents the dog's teeth from getting near anyone's hand. Instead, you handle the dog's mouth. When the people have a lot of physical difficulty throwing a ball, it can be more satisfying to give each person two throws per turn. That way, each person is more likely to achieve at least one good throw each turn.

4. Use a tennis ball or other soft object. If a wild throw hits the dog or a person, a tennis ball is unlikely to cause harm. A tennis ball with a short rope drawn through it is perfect. You can make your own by cutting an "X" on each side of the ball and pushing the end of a straightened wire coat hanger all the way through. Bend the end of the coat hanger into a flat loop, thread the rope through the loop, and pull it back through the ball. Tie a loop for a handle on one side and a big knot on the other side of the ball. Save the coat hanger tool for making future ball toys.

5. In all retrieving play with your dog, avoid causing the dog

to jump up and land on just the hind legs. This landing is structurally unstable for a dog, and horrible injuries have resulted.

Some dogs are almost dainty when retrieving around people and you may not need all the precautions. Even these dogs may get more vigorous as they gain experience, so observe your dog and stay ready to add extra control.

Away from therapy dog visits, if you have several dogs, avoid excessive competition among them in retrieving or any other game. Provide plenty of objects for them all to retrieve or seek. Throw toys in different directions, and use each dog's name. Never throw one toy for multiple dogs to chase; that's asking for disaster.

If you can't get your dogs to cooperate, train them separately. With patience, you may get them to work together eventually. This is most convenient, as it lets you play impromptu games with the dogs without first having to separate them. If you can work and play with them in each other's presence, they will stimulate each other to learn.

Don't put off teaching a dog to retrieve because that dog is too intimidated to do it in front of your other dogs. Just do the retrieving work during your individual training sessions with the dog away from the house. Retrieving is super for a dog's working attitude, and is well worth your time to develop in your dog.

## TO TUG OR NOT TO TUG?

One game you may not want to play with your dog is tug-of-war. While some trainers use this game to build drive in competition dogs, it has little to offer the therapy or family dog. I used to play tug-of-war with my dogs, until Spirit taught me about dogs who can't handle it. When training Gabriel, I realized I truly prefer my therapy dogs to have no tug-of-war. Retrieving and gentle teasing are healthier and safer ways to learn the same lessons.

Some dogs are naturally dominant or highly prey-driven, and unless the owner is an expert, present special risks with tug-of-war. The game pits the dog's strength against the owner's, and can lead to other confrontations.

A child has no hope of real dominance with most dogs, and can get carried away with the game until the dog is overexcited. Allowing a child to play tug-of-war with a dog is not a good idea.

Another problem is when a dog wants to play tug-of-war all the time. This game should have, at most, a minor role in your interaction with your dog, and should be reduced as you and your dog find more interesting things to do together. If this isn't happening, take a close look at your tug-of-war games to make sure you aren't risking a dangerous confrontation. This is important because, as dogs age, their urge to become dominant increases. What was okay with a young dog may not be okay with the same dog at age two, four, six, or older. The aging dog is also more easily injured.

If you can't get the dog to surrender the article on your command, all tug-of-war games must stop. Not only is the game dangerous with such a dog, but you will also make the dog feel more dominant and will increase the risk of someone getting bitten.

Animating the object in order to make it more desirable and to "turn the dog on" is the true purpose of tug-of-war in dog training. It can help teach your dog to give things up to you when you say so, and can reinforce your control over your dog. If it ever becomes a real battle between you and your dog, stop.

Tug-of-war is not a good idea on therapy dog visits. It makes the dog look "tough," which is not an effective image for working around fragile people in health-care facilities. It puts the dog in a higher drive state than is desirable on therapy dog visits. Also, it can encourage people to try to get the dog to play tug-of-war with them, which is dangerous.

## INHIBITING THE BITE

*"Star, Close Your Mouth. GOOD Close Your Mouth!" When you first start this exercise with your dog, hold the back of the collar with your left hand to stabilize the head.*

Another important aspect of conditioning the therapy dog to handling is inhibiting the tendency to bite humans. Most families need this conditioning in their dogs, too. Unfortunately, many dog owners condition their dogs incorrectly regarding the use of teeth.

None of the techniques described here are for the dog geniunely intending to bite you. If this is the case with your dog, or if you have any fear of your dog, get the help of an expert dog trainer or behavior specialist before it's too late. This expert will need to interact with both your dog and your family in order to diagnose and solve the problem. Such a dog is not a therapy dog candidate.

If a puppy stays in its litter long enough, or has normal relationships with other dogs, it will learn from the other dogs not to bite too hard. Once a dog knows how to inhibit the bite with other dogs, it must learn a new standard for people. Tooth pressure comfortable for another dog can tear right through human skin. Your dog won't know this unless you teach it.

When a dog's tooth touches your hand, let your hand go limp. You could hurt yourself by yanking the hand away and scraping it on a tooth. Jerking could also stimulate the dog to grab onto your hand with its teeth. As you and your dog progress in conditioning to-gether, you may later want to introduce some jerking in order to condition the dog not to reflexively respond by grabbing, in case this happens on a therapy dog visit. Use caution.

One thing to try when a dog accidentally and playfully puts teeth on you is to "Yipe!" loudly, and shun the dog for about fifteen minutes. Dogs use this form of feedback with each other, but your tone

*The signal reminds Star to watch where she puts her teeth, and also serves as a "no barking" cue!*

of voice has to be just right, and not all dogs respond well to it. Some will get wilder with their teeth, thinking it's an exciting game.

How my dogs have learned to inhibit the bite reveal typical situations and methods you can use at home.

The easiest were Angel, a female miniature American Eskimo, and Gabriel, a male Belgian Tervuren. Both were already strongly inhibited against biting humans when I adopted them. Angel was about eighteen months old, Gabriel a couple of months older. Both dogs responded instantly to verbal reminders. Training of all kinds progressed quickly as a result.

Saint, half Labrador and half German shepherd, was a tender-mouthed retriever, an instinct selectively bred into some dogs so they won't damage game. Saint only bit down on food or toys. As soon as he felt a hand in his mouth, he pulled his teeth away from it.

When we got Saint from the city animal shelter at a rowdy nine months of age, his biggest problem was swinging his open mouth around and accidentally bumping us with his teeth. Our "yiping" solved the problem. He would rather have died than hurt us.

A related problem came with his mania for retrieving. He liked to play tug-of-war, too, but for him it was just an appetizer to retrieving. In play, he would carelessly bump our hands with his teeth.

I taught Saint a special command called Close Your Mouth. I held his collar at the back of his neck with my left hand, encircling his muzzle with my right hand and holding it shut for about fifteen seconds, while saying "Saint, Close Your Mouth. Good Close Your Mouth!"

Don't pinch the dog's lip or tongue against its teeth. Making this manipulation painful for the dog could make it dangerous for you. Hold the dog just beyond the time it protests and then settles. Don't release the dog when it's struggling, but don't hold it for five minutes, either.

Having the mouth restrained, even with praise, is slightly unpleasant for the dog. Saint liked to avoid it whenever he could. Therefore he quickly learned to respond to the command, or to my signal of forming my right hand into a backward "C" shape. The same command and signal will tell a dog to stop barking. Remember, this is a restraint, not a violent or painful correction.

Star, a Belgian Tervuren, presented a more complicated situation. She was extremely submissive, active, obedient and loving, yet bred to use gentle nipping and holding to control sheep. Star frequently nipped and gripped my other dogs. They didn't mind it at all, nor did it harm them.

But of course Star couldn't be allowed to nip and grip people. Teaching her not to was complicated by the fact that she knew she wasn't hurting me, so didn't believe my "yipe." And it was a strong instinct. She had an enormous drive to interact with me by touching with her teeth.

She easily learned the Close Your Mouth, but didn't quickly stop touching me with her teeth as Saint had. I had to keep telling her. One helpful correction was to hold her upper jaw for fifteen seconds with my hand whenever she mouthed me. The idea was if she put her mouth on me, I'd take it away for awhile. It helped without traumatizing her, but it wasn't enough.

With an aggressive dog a more severe correction might have been in order, but tough corrections don't work well with soft dogs. They get so upset they can't think, and then all they learn is not to trust you. Therefore, I decided to try an approach often effective with an undesirable expression of an instinct:  redirect the dog's behavior. When you correct a dog harshly for expressing a strong instinct, you risk destroying the behavior in the dog completely, and damaging the dog's working ability. It's better to teach the dog a different response to use whenever the problematic instinct is stimulated inappropriately.

I taught Star a word for licking. Then, whenever I saw her want to put teeth on me, I told her to "kiss" instead. She got to respond to what her herding-dog nature craved, and I got an acceptable behavior from her. I think of this technique as "Seal It with a Kiss"!  The potentially problematic instinct terminates in a safe, gentle gesture. Believer, who at seven months was constantly touching our hands with her teeth, learned even faster than Star did. Perhaps this was because we had a plan in place when she first came!

These examples illustrate only a few possible situations. If you get your dog as a puppy, you can inhibit the bite at a younger age. We went through this with Spirit, whose drive to nip was beyond anything I had ever seen, though, like Star, she never caused injury. Using Close Your Mouth to the age of ten months, we produced a dog that no longer even thinks about putting teeth on humans. With her defensive and over-reactive temperament, bite inhibition training likely saved her life, even though it could not make a therapy dog of her.

Letting a puppy or dog bite humans, even in play, leads to serious problems. In the long run, your dog's life may be at stake, and certainly its therapy dog work.

## TEASING AS A FORM OF PLAY

Teasing is often involved in play with dogs. While having fun, a dog is in the ideal mental state to learn, and won't be especially sensitive to pain. Playful, thoughtful teasing can increase a dog's tolerance for handling and improve both your control over the dog and the dog's self-control. If at any time in a game the dog stops having fun, then the game has gone too far.

Teasing must never become abusive to the dog, nor to the person teasing. In play, the dog can learn what hurts people and what doesn't, how to move safely around people and other lessons. Work up to it gradually, and use good judgement.

Do not allow children to tease your dog. Children cannot be expected to know what is appropriate teasing and what is not. They can get hurt, and they can ruin good dogs. Men who like to play roughly with dogs can create problems for therapy dogs, too.

Teasing is used to train protection and guard dogs. You don't want your therapy dog made inappropriately aggressive by teasing. This can also happen when a dog is kept chained outdoors. People and other animals pass by, just out of reach, and the dog wants more and more to get at them. Then one day something goes wrong with the chain or the collar, or someone resembling somebody who's been teasing the dog comes within reach, and the dog acts out the overstimulated defense drive. This is also why it's vital to make sure no one teases your dog over the backyard fence.

One of the most valuable uses of teasing, as long as you can maintain control, is getting the dog really worked up and then helping it to exercise self-control. At this point you can also work on inhibiting the bite. When the dog wants to put its teeth on you, show it what to do instead (Seal it with a kiss!). Never do this with a dog you don't know well.

Keep teasing fun for both you and the dog. Never risk letting it get out of control, and never carry it on too long. Dogs get worked up as they play longer and longer. They get tired at the same time, and may miss and bite you by accident, or injure themselves. For the same reason, if dogs seem to be getting too wild playing with each other, make them take a break.

## ALL KINDS OF SIGHTS, SCENTS AND SOUNDS

Therapy dogs need to be as un-afraid of the world around them as possible. Dogs vary in their reactions to stimuli. Some dogs, like my Belgian Ter-vuren, bred for in-stantly noticing stray sheep, are highly stimulated by what they see. Other dogs are more tuned to scent. Typical of the

*Help your dog learn to ride calmly in a car, so it will arrive at the destination ready to work. Teach the dog never to jump out of a car without permission.*

Labrador side of his genetics, Saint needed to sniff things in order to fully "see" them. And many dogs are sensitive to noises, either genetically or due to frightening experiences. Dogs can have a combination of sensitivities. Acute senses are not a problem for a therapy dog. The dog's reactions to things it senses are what matter.

Generally the more experience your dog has with things the better, as long as the experiences are positive. Whenever your dog shows a negative reaction to anything, you want to work to give the thing a positive or neutral meaning in the dog's view. For example, you drop a pan in the kitchen and the dog runs yelping from the room. Chasing the dog with the pan to show it the pan is harmless may only make things worse.

I might start by setting the pan down on the floor and going to the dog. I bring the dog to an upbeat and happy state of mind with my voice, with play, or whatever else I know works for the particular dog. My goal is to excitedly induce the dog to accompany me back into the kitchen and have a happy time there, with the pan still on the floor. This will be enough for the first session.

In future sessions, using obedience commands, I will have the dog at a distance from the pan when it is dropped—whatever distance keeps the dog from feeling panic. If working alone, I might throw the pan away from the dog. I could tether the dog on a Stay and walk away, then throw the pan even further away. A quick way to get a strong retrieving dog to overcome sensitivity to an object is simply to let the dog fetch it to you.

Eventually I will work the dog up to being able to remain calm at the closest safe distance from the pan when it is dropped. Obviously it would be counterproductive to drop the pan where it could bounce up and hit the dog; then the dog would be right to run out of the room yelping! The dog would trust me less in future when I tell it something is safe.

Gabriel is a sensitive dog who tends to move away when startled. Then he quickly recovers and is willing to come right back and investigate the stimulus. He does not react with aggression, or with blind, out-of-control panic. A dog's temperament is an intricate constellation, with no one factor determining success or failure. You need to discover what works best for your dog, and become, over time, an expert in those maneuvers. Then the two of you can handle anything together.

Gabriel responds beautifully to "jolly talk," in which I cheer him on as we approach something together. Also, as a herding dog, he is more inclined to feel positively about something if he can follow it. When big rolling objects being moved through the nursing home startled him early in his career, I would jolly-talk him as they passed to help him hold his ground, then we would follow the object together. This has had marvelous results, without causing any setbacks to his work along the way. If you want to use this technique, remember to follow the object with the dog, but not chase it. Getting the dog too tuned in to predatory instincts would create a whole new problem!

Concerning scents, you'll help your dog a lot just by a life indoors with access to people's activities in your bathroom, kitchen and all the other rooms in the house. When a dog sniffs something you don't want it to touch, use a command and praise to redirect the dog. Avoid giving the dog a negative impression about any scent. Be matter-of-fact, let the dog sniff briefly if feasible, and help your dog learn to take all kinds of smells in stride. You might be surprised what your dog will encounter inside a typical household over a couple of years.

A dog's initial reaction to a strange sight, scent or sound may be defensive—to face it down or run from it. You can soften any defensive responses to new stimuli through positive experiences with all sorts of safe situations. In spite of your best efforts, you will sometimes miss the valid reasons your dog has for fearing things. For example, I noticed Gabriel was a bit shy of the refrigerator, so I started feeding him next to it. He became comfortable about it, but after a couple of years, I accidentally bopped his lowered head with the refrigerator door when I opened it while he was eating. I had never realized the door was coming so close to his head!  With his well-established confidence, he swooped right back to the food dish as soon as the door was out of the way. Even though he had a good reason to shy from the door, it isn't likely to actually injure him, and he has learned to tolerate it nicely due to a strong positive stimulus—dinner!

The better you know your dog through games, training, cuddling, and living together, the more power you develop for handling. We specifically accustom therapy dogs to medical equipment and other typical sights, sounds and smells encountered in the work, but you will encounter new things throughout your dog's career. Your teamwork is the key to managing your dog through new situations. I find these partnerships endlessly fascinating and satisfying. Each of my dogs has needed different handling from me. The handler's job is to have the knowledge and skill for this therapy dog, in this situation.

## CORRECTION

*Here's a perfect example of body language correcting a dog. Star was finely tuned to a smiling handler, so Bill's making a face at her was a correction!*

Sometimes it's proper to physically discipline a dog, though not nearly as often as people do it. This enters into conditioning to handling, whether by plan or by accident. Some dogs in obedience training, for example, learn to tolerate neck-jerk collar corrections. Other dogs become increasingly intolerant of such corrections. Dogs have different body sensitivities; what is comfortable for one dog may be abusive for another. A major problem, too, is correction given by a poor trainer. If the correction is poorly timed, unfair, or too violent, the stress on the dog is greatly increased.

Dogs, like humans, need motivation in order to learn and to work. Corrections provide no motivation. Corrections can stop some bad behavior patterns, but they don't create good ones. Whatever motivator you use to teach something—food, praise, petting or play—will need to be given occasionally, forever. How long would you work without any reward or thanks? You would lose heart, and so would your dog.

Physical correction should only be used in the mildest form necessary to stop the dog from misbehaving. Violent corrections only *seem* to train a dog more quickly, when in fact they create new problems. There are no shortcuts to good training.

All corrections must be scaled to the size and sensitivities of the dog. Never give a physical correction when you are angry. If you must do something in anger, just yell. When you are angry your reflexes are impaired. A proper correction to a dog demands flawless timing. A little humor doesn't hurt either.

Always teach the dog what action you want, in place of the action you're correcting. If you don't know how you want the dog to behave in a particular situation, you're not ready to make a correction! You can destroy your dog's temperament and working ability with poor corrections.

Some dogs shouldn't be corrected by anyone other than their owners. If you have such a dog, you have the responsibility and the right to prohibit others from correcting it. If another person, even an obedience instructor, corrects your dog inappropriately, your dog's working ability may be ruined. You may be able to rehabilitate the dog through a long conditioning process, or you may not. No one has the right to inflict this on you and your dog.

If you are the kind of gentle, upbeat handler so needed in therapy dog work, your dog will become more sensitive to its handler, tuning in to your subtle methods.

An excellent method of correction for a therapy dog is to have the dog repeat an action it didn't perform properly. If necessary, give the dog more help the second time. When using this technique of boring repetition as a correction, let the dog stop after performing the action correctly. Remember to give generous praise.

An effective physical correction is to set up the situation to cause a dog to meet with some undesirable consequence if it disobeys. One example is to turn and go the other way if your dog is pulling on the leash. Another is to walk near a post when the dog is totally ignoring you on an on-leash walk. The dog will wind up on the wrong side of the post and realize the leash can tangle.

Helping the dog learn to solve the problem of being on the wrong side of the post is another useful therapy dog training opportunity, by the way. It's amazing to watch a dog figure out how to untangle its own leash. You can also, with patience, teach your dog to untangle the leash from around its own legs. I use the command "Fix It." Just say the words every time you untangle the leash from your dog's legs, and one day the dog will pick up the feet and untangle without your help.

Your body language is an excellent way to correct your dog, because dogs live in a world of body language. You can glare at your dog, shake your finger, stamp your foot, etc. Be sure to give lots of positive body language, instantly, when your dog behaves correctly. Soon you will be able to cue your dog to praise or correction with small changes in your facial expression.

You may feel like "staying mad," but the dog needs your immediate positive feedback when it has switched to the correct behavior. In the process, you will develop better control over your own emotions.

Another important aspect of correction is how you use the word "no." A roared "No!!!" is a severe correction to stop my dogs in their tracks. This is for emergencies, not to be thrown around carelessly until it has no meaning or browbeats the dog. The tone changes the word. For "not now," I say a soft "no," or "no-no." For "That was the wrong choice; try again," I say "no-o-o-o," drawing the word out into almost a question at the end.

You will also want to teach your dog specific "No" words, such as Leave It. Leave It means "don't touch it," and is an essential command for therapy dogs. More than once I have used Leave It to stop my dog from picking up a pill or even a sharp medical tool lying on the floor on a therapy dog visit. A bee, a strange dog, and food someone is trying to give your dog are all occasions for Leave It. You teach Leave It by saying the word, moving abruptly away from the item with your dog on leash, and praising the dog for moving with you. Occasionally add petting, a treat, or a game with you to give emphasis to your praise.

It's also wise to condition your dog to a correction sound. I like a squawking, buzzer-like "Aaaaa!" sound. When you give a correction, make this sound to condition the dog to eventually turn to you on just the sound, at which point you must quickly give the dog a new command and praise for obeying it. In the early stages, add extra reward after the praise, so your dog will learn to come out of a correction expecting something great to do with you next. This will save you from creating in your dog a defensive reaction to correction, and is a wonderful foundation when training a puppy.

Other specific correction words help your dog understand exactly what you want. I teach "Off the Bed" before allowing the dog access to the bed. "Out of there" or "Out of here" send a dog out of the kitchen when I've broken a glass item, or I'm waxing the floor. "Off the Cat" is pretty self-explanatory! "Off the Paper" is handy when I'm reading the newspaper on the floor or bed. "Let Him Go" is Spirit's command for taking teeth off Gabriel's collar because I just combed his hair for the therapy dog visit! These commands are followed by praise for the dog's compliance.

The therapy dog needs at least ten times as much reward as it gets correction, preferably much more. It needs this same ten-to-one (or greater) proportion of positive touch over negative touch in order to develop and maintain the proper response to being touched. To minimize the number of corrections you give, teach the dog what you want, rather than what you don't want. Then the dog gets praised, and your problem gets solved. This approach creates a more confident dog and your training will take the minimum amount of time, since you won't waste time rehabilitating problems created by excessive corrections.

*When Saint was 9, I began grooming him daily, to see if it would yield more benefits than daily cuddling, and grooming only as needed. The results were astonishing. However obedient and loving your dog is already, it will become more so with this small investment of your time. It also desensitizes the dog to occasional uncomfortable touch, making it far more likely to cope well with therapy dog work.*

## A CUDDLE A DAY

Find time to cuddle your dog every day. We all get busy, and it's easy to neglect this. I recommend combing, brushing, or rubbing down your dog to thoroughly groom it every day, with extra cuddling time. Watching television is a great time to groom and cuddle your dog.

Lots of people will pet your dog on therapy dog visits, and many will do it incorrectly. To offset this, your dog needs plenty of pleasant petting from friendly strangers. But most of all, your dog needs it from you. Your petting is the gold standard for your dog. No matter what a "love everybody" dog it is, there is no substitute for your love.

Dog owners with multiple dogs often say they can't pet or praise one dog without another getting jealous. My dogs know I won't tolerate competition near me. It's too dangerous for dogs to lash out at each other, even in otherwise-acceptable dog discussions, when right next to a human. If you live intimately with a group of dogs, you've seen a dominant dog flash lightning fast at a submissive one, and the submissive one knows just how and when to dodge, as if they were dancing. These interactions are sometimes playful, sometimes symbolic.

Even though my dogs don't fight with each other, if they played too near a person, the person could easily get bitten or knocked down, which is not at all what the dogs intended. It's unsafe for dogs to fight or play with each other on therapy dog visits. Yet in order to maintain good social abilities, dogs benefit from expressing these normal dog-to-dog behaviors at appropriate times.

One way to teach multiple dogs to interact at a safe distance from people is to banish them from your immediate presence whenever they roughhouse too near you. If they're on the bed with you, it's "Off the bed!" Send them all away. Don't attempt to determine who said what!

When you praise or pet one dog and another comes up wanting to join in, include both dogs. This greatly reduces competition for your attention and seems to build a team spirit. They all get praise and petting when any one of them earns it. Knowing this, they often become less needy and more content to wait for your attention. After the dogs learn to cooperate for cuddling, you'll find you can give a loving look or word to one dog across the room while holding another, making both happy. You may also find they seem pleased when they see you pet the other dogs.

During daily grooming and cuddling sessions, you can condition your therapy dog to handle many necessary aspects of interaction with people. Teaching a dog to tolerate people in its face is essential in order to work your dog with young children. Since this can be dangerous, proceed with the conditioning cautiously. Wait until you know the dog and have control over it before starting.

When you first put your face next to the dog's face, or any time you do it suddenly, the dog may react instinctively, and treat you as it would treat another dog. Dogs gnaw and snap and otherwise handle other dog faces in ways we humans can't endure. Cuddling time is a natural time for you to show your therapy dog how to behave around people's faces.

When a dog rises, the head leads, and can pack a wallop! Until the dog gets used to moving around people, the impact can accidentally give you a split lip or other injury. An easy way to handle this is to keep your hand on the top of the dog's head or the back of its neck.

Many people in facilities can't control their movements. Your dog will encounter people who don't know how to move around a dog, or who fear dogs and telegraph this through their movements. By playing with your dog at cuddling time, you can get it used to all sorts of human movements. End each disturbing movement with something the dog likes, such as tummy rubbing or a kiss.

In all conditioning of your dog to handling, remember your goal of teaching the dog to read people and to interact with them. Start by using good "dog language" to relate to your dog, then gradually accustom the dog to human language and behavior. Work your way up to hugging your dog, kissing its face, and touching it while it's eating. If other people are ever to be able to interact with your dog in these ways safely, you must practice them regularly. These must not be challenges for dominance between person and dog. They must become easy, give-and-take communications.

The time you spend regularly cuddling your therapy dog is even more important than training time. Through cuddling, you bond the dog to yourself. Training also creates bonds, but sometimes we make mistakes in training and push the dog too hard. Cuddling time repairs this damage. Spending regular time cuddling your dogs actually makes them more obedient.

Therapy dogs must be in good grooming condition whenever they visit facilities. Daily grooming makes it easy to get the dog ready for a visit, and also makes everybody want to pet the clean dog from day-to-day, thus giving the dog important conditioning for dog visits. Petting a dog lowers a human's blood pressure, and it even eases the pain of arthritis. A cuddle a day is good medicine!

# THERAPY DOGS

# 6

# BASIC CONTROL FOR THERAPY WORK

Much of the progress in therapy dog work has come through trainers who participate in the sport of obedience competition. Clarifying the differences between competition training and therapy dog training can make this relationship smoother and more productive. Obedience competition is a sport. Training and handling for therapy dog visits is neither a sport nor is it competitive. Therapy dog work is a volunteer job, rather than a dog activity or title.

Typically, a potential therapy dog will be neither defiant nor tough. Yet some of the best competition dogs are both, as are a large percentage of dogs brought to instructors for civilizing. Many dog-training techniques were derived from the training of tough and dominant dogs for police and military work. All of this means a particular trainer's curriculum can be wrong for you and your therapy dog.

I have found the drives theory from Jack and Wendy Volhards's *The Canine Good Citizen* and *Dog Training for Dummies* to be tremendously helpful. The instinctive drive your dog is in when working makes a difference. For therapy dog work, prey and defense drives can create problems. I work to build the pack drive in each therapy dog and to keep the dog in this drive as much as

*Humane training for control brings handler and dog together in a true partnership. Obedience exercises used in other types of training are effective for therapy dogs, too, but are often best taught to therapy dogs in different ways, due to the different nature of their work.*

possible on facility visits.

Another way trainers refer to drive is "high drive." A high state of drive looks good in competition and provides bursts of dog energy for the handler to shape. During therapy dog work, I want the dog in a low state of drive—a lower "gear." In this mode, the dog is calmer and can comfortably work longer. Therapy dog visits tend to last an hour or more, as opposed to the few intense minutes a dog works during a competition.

Your training techniques will affect the drive (prey, pack, defense flight and defense fight in the useful Volhard theory) the same command will elicit in your dog later. The dog will also tend to work in a high or low "gear," according to how you have trained. If you want to work the same dog in competition and in therapy dog work, I recommend training specifically and separately for the two different roles. Then you can have the high-energy response to your commands for the competition arena, and the calm response for therapy dog visits. If you can keep the different training and handling techniques straight (which is harder than it sounds!), the dog usually can, too.

## FINDING HELP

Before you can get good behavior from your dog, you must decide what behavior you want. Training takes time. If you don't set clear goals and work methodically toward them, the same length of time will pass, and your dog will still not be trained!

Your goals will change as you learn. For example, few people who enroll in a training class for the first time plan to enter their dogs in obedience or agility competitions. A small percentage of them get "hooked" and go into the sport. In the process, they usually get a wonderful education in dog handling, making the time spent worthwhile.

Another important reason to have goals is to recognize when you have progressed. Goals let you say, "I set out to accomplish that, and I succeeded!" This sense of achievement is emotionally healthy for you. You'll give your dog extra love and attention for helping you, which is great for the dog. Set short-term and small goals, as well as long-term and large goals, so you can celebrate often.

Once you have goals in mind, you're prepared to start seeking help with training. To train a therapy dog, you aren't looking for someone to train the dog for you. You'll need to thoroughly understand your dog. You'll need to develop handling skills for all situations, and you'll need to maintain the training for the rest of your dog's life.

Therefore, you're seeking an instructor to teach you. Obedience class is the best place for most handlers and dogs to start. Obedience club classes are usually affordable and humane. You will teach the therapy dog, with the instructor's help. The training should help prepare you to choose and train other dogs in the future.

One approach to training is to go to fun matches, classes and other dog events under the guidance of a private instructor. This individual help may be necessary for success if the class instruction in your area leaves something to be desired for therapy dog work. Evaluating the competence of an instructor is difficult for a beginning dog trainer. Choose an instructor carefully, and be sure to discuss your goals with this person (see the appendix for more information). Your training for therapy dog work may be impossible to achieve in certain classes, depending on their goals and methods.

Two other options are attending seminars and reading books. When presenting a seminar, the instructor can't fully interact with or thoroughly know you or your dog. Inappropriate training can ruin your dog. Seminars can be great, though, if you carefully evaluate new ideas before incorporating them into the way you handle your dog.

The same goes for books. Few books will be completely right for your situation, but the hundreds of dog books available offer a tremendous resource. To incorporate different points of view and avoid overlooking anything, seek out at least three books to help you formulate a training plan.

Armed with your goals, you're ready to evaluate an obedience class, private trainer, seminar or book to decide if it's right for you.

Here are some questions to consider:

1. What kind of dogs has this trainer (or writer) owned? This is more important than students' dogs in classes, because instructors don't get to know class dogs as well. A trainer's philosophy and the techniques he or she uses will be based more on the type of dogs he or she has owned than on any other factor. You need someone who owns the same general type of dog you do. It doesn't have to be the same breed. Important similarities can be grouped: guard dogs, sled dogs, herding dogs, terriers, large dogs, small dogs, shy dogs, assertive dogs, sensitive dogs, responsive dogs, retrievers, dogs bred to do the same type of work as your breed and other factors you consider important to understanding your dog. Look for someone who understands and loves your kind of dog.

2. Has this trainer or writer participated in the work you plan to do with your dog? Is he or she still active in the work? Do you respect and admire the trainer's efforts in this field?

3. In observing the trainer, are you comfortable with the way dogs are treated? If not, walk away, close the book, take your dog home!

4. Can you communicate well with this instructor? If the instructor intimidates you, your goals may never be considered. You must remain in control of how people treat your dog.

5. What do other dog handlers whose opinions you respect think of this instructor? Dog people love to talk about dogs and training ideas. Don't be shy about calling, writing or approaching another trainer politely in public and asking for help. (Be cautious when approaching people at competitive dog events. They might rebuff you out of nervousness. Matches are usually more relaxed and better places to meet people and ask questions.) Talking to other dog people can be your best means of finding the right instructor in your community to help you and your dog.

## BASIC PRINCIPLES

You'll need to seek specific help with your dog, and one book isn't enough to tell you how to train your dog. But this book would not be complete without a description of the basic control exercises a therapy dog and handler need to know, and at least one appropriate way to teach them to a therapy dog. Be sure to tailor this advice to your dog.

Two important ideas are central to therapy dog training, and initiative is the first. The therapy dog will ideally learn to think for itself and to share its thoughts with you. Initiative is also called intelligent disobedience or responsibility. Initiative is a factor in the training of many working dogs, including assistance dogs for people with disabilities, police dogs, hunting dogs and herding dogs.

Whenever people depend on a dog's senses, which are more acute than human senses, the dog needs initiative. Sometimes the dog's senses will tell it your command is wrong, according to what the responsible dog has learned you actually want. To take full advantage of your dog's abilities in therapy dog work, you need to develop the dog's initiative, while still keeping good control. It's a fascinating challenge.

The second basic principle is: Never correct your dog when it's in the act of being friendly. You may intend the correction for some other misdeed, but doing it when a dog is in the act of being friendly risks your dog's good attitude toward interacting with people. Interacting with people is a therapy dog's job, so you certainly want to preserve all aspects of this ability, including the dog's attitude.

This principle also applies when the dog is acting friendly toward another dog. This doesn't mean letting your dog bother others. Instead, redirect the dog's attention. Neither punish nor correct your dog at any time the dog might experience the correction as a negative result of a friendly attitude. This is an example of correcting for one behavior and accidentally creating a problem with another.

These two ideas are essential for training your dog to initiate communication with people and respond to them. Some dogs will never learn to make responsible decisions if allowed to take initiative. Such dogs may not be the best prospects for therapy dogs, but can often be worked with meticulous training and handling. Trainers who believe in training dogs strictly to obey, never to make independent decisions, likely own this kind of dog. The kind of dog you have will determine the appropriate training and handling techniques.

The following exercises are not difficult to master, if you practice regularly and properly. Problems arise when trainers try to accomplish through severe corrections what they should have accomplished through practice. A dog treated in such an unfair manner can become traumatized and unreliable. Rehabilitating the dog takes longer than training properly in the first place, and is not always possible.

Keep practice sessons short and interesting for you and the dog. Five to twenty minutes is right for most dogs. Two or three short sessions a day can be effective. Interspersing play with training will enhance your control.

As training progresses, go for outings with your dog and mix training in along the way. Then you and your dog will develop the habit of maintaining control for an hour or more at a time, which obedience classes and therapy dog visits require.

The techniques described here are for dogs with temperaments suited to therapy dog work. Handling is designed to be acceptable in a health-care setting or a highly public place. Nonconfrontational methods are used because therapy dogs need to relate to their handlers and the people they serve in a nonconfrontational manner. Touch is integral to the training here, because therapy dogs must be comfortable with touch at any point during their work. Therapy dog work is different from any other dog job, and the most effective and efficient training for therapy dog work is different from other dog training, too.

Many past therapy dogs have been trained for other things before becoming therapy dogs. In fact, this was the case with my own first three therapy dogs. Today experienced handlers are training successor dogs specifically for therapy dog work, and new handlers are starting their dog training with this as their goal. It is more important than ever to define therapy dog training, in order to prepare dogs and handlers to the optimum level of ability with a minimum of counterproductive effort.

## COME

The first command to teach your dog is to Come when called. The attention work discussed in Chapter 5, "Attention, Release" is the best introduction you can give your dog to coming when called. Any reward you use in the attention exercise will help your recall work, too. Keep the reward out of sight until you have first praised the dog, and don't always give the same reward. As your dog progresses, praise and petting will be enough reward for the recall almost every time. It's ideal if you occasion-

*A line with no tension on it, happy body language from Bill, and here comes Gabriel in a joyful response to the Come command.*

ally add a surprise reward, giving the dog reason to believe a special reward is always a possibility. Gabriel knows he may get a special treat if he leaves off barking at a squirrel to run to me quickly!

To start, decide on a command word for Come, and use it only when you can make sure the dog will come to you. In other situations when you wish to call your dog but it is not imperative that your dog comes, don't use the command word. Instead, you can say "Puppy, puppy, puppy!" or the dog's name in an excited voice. You can say "Cookie!" or some other reward word your dog knows, but always keep this promise, or soon the word won't work anymore. Save "Come" strictly for when you're prepared to make sure the dog obeys. This goes for all command words, if you want your dog to understand them as true commands.

Train your dog to the point of reliably carrying out each action from a single command. On therapy dog visits, continuous verbal encouragement from you is a plus, and it may occasionally be appropriate to repeat a command. In training, make sure your dog understands that it is a command the first time you give it.

Puppies instinctively follow and come to their owners. Typically, dog owners call their dogs to punish them, to put them in carriers, to put medicine in their ears, and other things dogs don't like. Most people also punish their dogs when they catch them after they have gotten loose. Not surprisingly, most dogs don't come when called—humans have taught them to run! Your recall training will go far more smoothly if you don't make this common mistake.

To start teaching a command for coming when called, have your dog on leash. Any line attached to a secure collar will do. Say the dog's name, pause slightly after the name, then the command word: "Gabriel, Come!"

Your tone of voice depends on the dog. Try a soft tone for a soft dog, a deeper pitch for a more brassy dog, a higher pitch for a small dog. Save yelling for emergencies, not dog training. You'll learn what your dog responds to best as you work together. Experiment and listen to yourself. Notice the dog's reactions to different voice tones. Before starting therapy dog visits, you'll have to learn to elicit responses from the dog with commands given in a pleasant voice, without physical corrections. It saves time to train with such tones and handling from the start.

If the dog doesn't come when you call and doesn't respond to body language when you kneel down, spread your arms or run the other way, tug, then loosen the line to get the dog started.

Encourage and praise as the dog comes to you. If the tug-and-release doesn't get the dog started, keep a good humor and reel the dog in, or go to the dog and lead it back with you. When you say "Come," get the dog to you, whether on its own or by putting its body through the motions.

Losing your temper is counterproductive, since pain and fear both

*The long line lets you work your dog on commands at a distance, without putting the dog or anyone else at risk by having it loose in the open during training.*

interfere with a dog's learning. The less tugging the better, because it distracts the dog from what you want it to understand. Enthusiastically praise and pet the dog after it reaches you, no matter how hard you had to work to get it there.

Try your dog off leash when the dog is completely consistent on leash. If the off-leash dog tries to evade you, go back to working on leash for several weeks. A twenty to forty-foot line will let you practice distance around distractions, without risking a loose dog.

The recall requires long-term, consistent training. If you call your dog and it doesn't come, get up from your easy chair and go get the dog. Never give a command when you are not prepared to follow through on it. Let's look at some real-life examples.

One day I was walking in my neighborhood with one of my dogs on leash and saw two elderly men calling a loose dog. The dog was a clever Border Collie I knew. He wasn't near traffic, nor was he fleeing in panic; he was moving in a big, Border Collie circle! I think he had been trained in a former home. The rather frail men were chasing the dog as best they could, yelling threats at him. I'll bet the dog was able to evade them until they were too tired to carry out their threats.

Another day I was indoors when my dogs began barking. I looked out the window and saw a Chow romping in my front yard, followed by two frightened girls. One was carrying a leash. The dog was heading toward a busy four-lane street, responding to the girls only by moving away from them. I opened the window and told the girls to try running away from the dog. They did, and the dog stopped going toward the dangerous street, which gave me time to get outside. The dog came up to me curiously, and without touching it I talked to it in a happy voice and walked it back to the now-kneeling girls, who then put on the leash.

I used to take my three dogs in the car on cool mornings for Saint to work a scent track. The other two dogs knew they would be staying in the car. One morning Angel decided to lead a play expedition with her faithful sidekick, Star. When I opened the car door, both dogs jumped out and took off across the empty parking lot.

My first instinct was to scream at them and chase them. But then my training kicked in, and I stopped. I called to them in my happiest voice. They whirled around and came to me. I praised them for coming. I encouraged them back into the car, and I did not punish them. Ever since then, I've been extra careful to put the dog back in the car for another try whenever any of my dogs jumps out without permission, even in the garage or when I have already put on the leash and we're getting out for a therapy dog visit. In the garage, I often fling the door open as might happen if I jumped out of the car for some sort of emergency, and praise the dog for staying in spite of such temptation. An off-leash recall out in the open, possibly in traffic, is not a skill I want to test, if I can prevent it.

As these examples show, if your dog isn't trained, you may be able to get the dog to come to you in an emergency, but you will first have to control your emotions and use the right handling! If your dog is trained, you can still fail by not using what you know and your dog's life could be the price of failure. In coming when called, as in all dog training, controlling ourselves is absolutely necessary if we wish to control our dogs.

## SIT-STAY

The next thing most educated dogs learn is the Sit-Stay. Teach this command gently. Treats can help in early training for the Sit, especially with a puppy. Just be sure you keep it hidden from view until time to give it to the dog.

To entice your puppy into a Sit, use a treat that you draw from the puppy's nose backward just above its head. Say "Good Sit." In subsequent sessions, say "Sit" first, and watch for that moment the puppy sits before you show the food. It won't take long!

If you've properly conditioned your dog to being handled, you can use physical manipulation to teach the dog what you mean by Sit. You can even sit beside the dog for early lessons. Be gentle. First the dog needs to learn what Sit means. Gradually you'll turn the conditioning into a command, and work with the dog on leash.

I like to put the dog into a Sit with two hands. The right palm pushes the chin up gently, while the left hand, palm downward, gently tucks the dog's rear. Don't push a dog's hips down forcefully, because you could injure the dog. If the dog is huge

Bill's right hand supports Star's chin while his left hand slides down over her rear. Avoid pushing down on a dog's hips, because your dog might have a physical problem you have not yet detected. Instead, tuck the rear into the Sit.

In this stronger control position, Bill's right thumb is hooked through Star's collar as his hand supports her chin. His left hand slips behind her knees, to "fold" her gently into the Sit.

The "traffic cop" signal works for Stay when you're standing in front of the dog.

or confused, slip the left hand down further, behind the knees to gently bend them and cause the dog to sit on your left palm. Pull your hand out at the last minute. You can hook your right thumb through the front of the dog's collar to help you steady the chin. Later your right palm moving upward (as it did under the chin) becomes a Sit signal.

Until the dog understands and any time later when it fails to obey the command, place it into position with your hands. As the dog progresses in the training, you can place the dog faster in order to speed up the response, and your touch will be light, largely symbolic. A therapy dog has to sit reliably on command, but not quickly, so whether or not you train for a fast response is optional.

When your dog understands the Sit command, start following sometimes with the Stay command, and gradually lengthen the time you require the dog to Sit. At this point you will need the leash, but keep it loose, no tension. You want the dog to respond to you, not to leash pressure. As you say "Stay," give a hand signal. When standing at the dog's side, I hold my left hand, flat palm toward the dog with fingers together, just in front of the dog's nose. When you begin stepping out and turning to face the dog, you can reinforce your verbal Stay with a hand held out, palm toward the dog, in a traffic-cop style gesture.

Remain right in front of the dog for a long period of the Stay training, gradually beginning to step and hop around, make funny noises, and otherwise help the dog learn to remain in place. Stay means Stay. With you several feet away, it takes too long to put the dog back in position when it breaks. The delay thoroughly confuses the dog as to the meaning of the Stay command. Your ideal reaction is to notice the dog beginning to move, and get it to settle back before it actually even breaks position, preferably without touching the dog.

Use a watch, or count the time silently ("One thousand, two thousand," etc.). It might take three months or so of daily practice to work up to two minutes at thirty feet, and longer for a puppy. Eventually a five-minute Sit-Stay, with you going out of sight, is a good goal for an advanced therapy dog. This might take several months of practicing every day, and a mature dog.

For a Stay longer than five minutes, it's best to leave your dog in a Down rather than a Sit. The Sit position is somewhat uncomfortable for a dog to maintain. On a slippery floor, such as those often found in facilities, a seated dog has to continually work to keep its front feet from sliding forward.

Keep your attention on the dog throughout any Stay exercise. Handler attention is one of the secrets of success in dog training, and takes practice and effort to develop in yourself. You will need this skill on therapy dog visits.

If your dog is conditioned to your voice, verbal encouragement and praise will help it learn to Stay. Praise the dog when it is steady, and caution the dog when it starts to break without permission ("No, Stay."). Learn to recognize when your dog is about to move, and learn to react in time. These skills are vital in therapy dog work.

During practice, I prefer to have the dog Stay until after I return, stand beside it for fifteen seconds and release. This conditions the dog to wait for my command, rather than break out of the Stay when it thinks I am going to give the command soon.

I command the dog to walk a few steps forward with me to end the Stay. Praise your dog during the Stay, and praise only mildly or not at all after the release. You want the dog to feel good about working, not about quitting.

Remember to end the Stay exercise when it's time, not when you see the dog about to break! If the dog is about to break, help it Stay. The extra fifteen seconds of holding the Stay after you return will help your dog avoid the fault of breaking the command too soon. Fiddle with the leash, pet the dog, and otherwise let it learn to stay until you release, in spite of any other action happening before the release.

If your dog breaks the Stay, simply put the dog back and restart the time. Don't punish the dog, or you might accidentally condition it to run from you when it breaks a Stay. On therapy dog visits the dog must sometimes move from a Stay. You don't want your dog to run, or to stay there and cause someone to fall when you didn't see the person coming. Dogs are much more alert to movement than people are. If you train carefully, your dog will learn to come calmly to you when it needs to break a Stay in real work.

If you see someone approaching to pet your dog, release the dog from command before it can break, unless you can nicely ask the person to wait until you finish the exercise. You can practice commands any time, but friendly helpers to pet your therapy dog aren't always available. If you think asking them to wait would turn them away, release the dog right then for petting, or move to the dog's side and hold it in position during petting.

Whenever your dog breaks the command before you can release it for petting, have the dog do the Stay again. Restart the clock so it gets no credit for the time it did stay. The extra time is the penalty. If you consistently time every Stay, your dog will fully recognize this penalty, due to a dog's keen sense of time. Don't punish or correct the dog for breaking a Stay to be friendly. Thank the person for helping you train your therapy dog!

As your Stay work progresses, you will gradually move farther away, and remove the leash, but don't rush either of these steps. Some types of dogs don't work well off leash. Teach such a dog the off-leash work anyway, always in a location where the dog can't get loose and into trouble. Then keep the dog on leash during therapy dog visits. The off-leash training will give you additional control. A long line allows you to practice Stays at a distance without taking your dog off-leash in the open.

If the dog's instincts or training aren't reliable for off-leash work, it's no problem for a therapy dog to remain on leash at all times on visits. Do what's best for your dog, even if other handlers take their dogs off leash. Some people take their dogs off leash because they can't control the dogs on leash. This is not an acceptable reason! Every therapy dog handler must be proficient at the skill of handling a dog on leash. There's no substitute for practice in learning this skill.

## DOWN-STAY

*Bill pushes gently downward and backward on Star's shoulders as he gives the Down signal and command. Don't push straight down on the shoulders. Another option is to lift the dog's front legs and gently lay them out in a Down position.*

Down-Stay is an excellent control position. The foundation for the Down-Stay is the time spent cuddling, handling, holding and petting your dog. If your dog has trouble with Stays, the cuddling time will be just as important as training time in achieving your eventual success. Another approach that greatly aids Stay training is the Long Down and Long Sit described in books (*The Canine Good Citizen*, and *Dog Training for Dummies*) by Jack and Wendy Volhard. This one-month program can be done at the same time you are teaching stays and other exercises, and truly works wonders.

To introduce your puppy to the Down command, draw a treat from the puppy's nose straight down to its front feet. When the puppy lies down so as better to reach the treat, release the food and say "Good Down!" Puppies find the Down a bit difficult, and my favorite trick for teaching it to them is simply to have them do a "Down" for each meal, before I put the dish on the floor. They learn fast!

Herding dogs have a specific command and whistle tone for the Down. They're taught to drop instantly at a distance from the handler when in the exciting act of chasing livestock. Similarly, competition dogs lose points for slow drops. Your therapy dog does not have to drop quickly. A herding dog drops

*Soon the signal and command will elicit the Down response from your dog.*

on natural turf, and a competition dog drops on grass or a rubber mat, but therapy dogs often have to drop on pavement or hard floors. Therefore, teach the therapy dog to Down from a Sit, which is easier and gentler than teaching it from running or standing. Later you can practice Downs in motion on soft surfaces, if you wish.

To teach the Down from the Sit, one end is already down, so you can gently push down and back on the shoulders, or pull the front legs forward. Never shove your dog down or yank the dog's legs out from under it. If the dog flops on its back, don't rub its tummy; that's why dogs roll over like this. In time the dog will gain confidence and stay more upright. As long as both ends remain down and in the same location, the dog is allowed to shift its weight. It must hold its position and remain facing the same direction (if the dog scoots, calmly but quickly scoot the dog back to the correct spot), but it may change weight from one hip to the other. There is no good reason to demand military precision when all you need is a steady, reliable Down-Stay.

Watch your tone on the Down command. A mean tone on this command is offensive in public and is the wrong handling for a therapy dog. You want the dog to obey happily, not be browbeaten into submission.

You can start the Down-Stay work soon after the Sit, and develop the time on them together. You can practice first the Sit and then the Down each day if you wish. Practice during your daily training, or at a convenient time, such as while preparing the dog's food or watching television. Keep attention on your dog to reposition immediately if it breaks, to restart the time if necessary, and to release the dog at the correct time. Work up to four minutes on the Down, ten minutes for an advanced, mature dog.

As you teach the word "Down," teach a signal, too. When I'm next to the dog, my Down signal is the first two fingers of my right hand extended, starting in front of the dog's nose and guiding it to the ground.

On both Sit- and Down-Stays, the out-of-sight work is accomplished gradually, and only when the dog is mature. Training for out-of-sight Stays is valuable for therapy dog work. You may occasionally use this skill on a visit and it will help your dog in therapy testing, though in both cases the dog may not actually have to do a perfect stay. What the training does is teach your dog that it's okay to stay when you are out of sight, and that you can be trusted to come back in a reasonable time. I recommend four minutes, since testing tends to be for three minutes.

Corners are useful when training out-of-sight Stays. You can be close but out of sight around a corner. In the earliest stage I enjoy setting up a mirror so the dogs and I can see each other in it. Taught this way, they always believe I'm just around the corner! Lacking a mirror, you can peek in and out from around the corner. You can also do this training effectively by using a window. At first, remain where the dog can see you, and over a number of training sessions, start ducking out of sight.

*Heel is a useful command whenever you and your dog must pass a distraction. For a particularly enticing distraction, make quick changes of direction to hold your dog's attention.*

## HEEL

Heel prepares your dog for the outside world. If your puppy isn't used to the leash, the first step is to introduce it as a pleasant, not scary, experience. Letting the puppy drag the leash helps, starting with short sessions and never letting the pup reach the point of panic. The first time you put the leash on and hold the other end, basically just follow the puppy. Encourage the pup to go the way you want to go, but use no force.

By far the easiest, fastest, and most fun way to teach a puppy or dog to heel is to use treats, given when the dog is in the correct position, moving with you, and looking at your face. It's simply the next step of the "Attention, Release" described in Chapter 5. Now instead of backing away from the dog, you reinforce the dog with the tiny treats for moving at your side in unison with you. Don't be afraid that this will make the dog dependent on treats for heeling. As with attention in general, you can switch to praise, petting, and sometimes a toy as your work progresses.

The perfect, total-attention heeling of the obedience ring is not necessary for therapy dog work. It's okay to teach it to your therapy dog if you wish, but use a different command for walking the dog without total attention, such as when your dog is relating to other people.

Heel refers to the dog's position, at your left side. If you're moving, Heel means to keep pace with you in that position. If you're stopped, Heel means to get to your left and to Sit. If you don't want the dog to Sit, you can give a different position command (such as Stand) as the dog reaches the Heel location. Teach the dog where Heel is in a positive manner. You want the dog to always feel secure next to you.

Keep your attention on the dog from the time you say "Heel" until you release the dog from command, even if in informal work you choose to let the dog look around a bit. It must pay enough attention to maintain position at your side, making this a useful command when you pass distractions. Heeling with intricate footwork, weaving around posts and turning in different directions while keeping the dog's attention will build your control.

Besides using Heel to take your dog's mind off a distraction, Heel is an excellent warm-up to calm an energetic dog before entering a facility. It shifts the dog into working gear. At its most sophisticated, heeling is like dancing with your dog. If you have trouble giving your dog steady foot movements to work with, you might try practicing with music.

As long as you're gentle with your dog, you can get as fancy with heeling as you like. If your dog forges ahead of you, go more slowly, stop often, make frequent about-turns and left turns, and back up now and then. If the dog tends to lag, walk more quickly in practice. Training too harshly for the dog's personality can cause lagging, so make sure you are not doing this. Heeling should be fun for the dog.

Heeling is much more difficult for the dog than it appears. Give lots of encouragement, and if you don't wish to train for precision, which would likely require some skillful coaching from an obedience expert, don't expect the dog to work with precision. Loose-lead walking is necessary for therapy dog work, but precision heeling is not.

When working your dog on leash, keep the leash loose as the base position. Anytime the leash goes tight, change directions, stop, or take some steps backwards to get the leash loose again. Make sure your arm holding the leash has the elbow in toward your body, with the arm bent rather than extended. This allows you to quickly get slack in the leash to change direction. When I see someone walking a dog with the arm pulled straight out by lead tension, I know the person lacks good control over the dog.

On a loose leash, your dog learns to respond to you. The training collar you need will be milder than when handler and dog habitually use a tight leash. On a tight leash, it takes a stiff pull to get the dog's attention. On a loose leash, it only takes a tweak. A tight leash can make your dog feel defensive, too, which is highly undesirable in a therapy dog.

When your dog has learned to Heel on leash, gradually teach the Heel off leash as well. You'll find this transition easy with a dog trained to give you attention on its name, to come when called, and to work on a loose leash. Even if you seldom use off-leash heeling on therapy dog visits, practicing it will increase your working rapport with your dog.

If you participate in competition obedience, I recommend separate commands for full-attention heeling and less precise loose-lead walking. I usually tell Gabriel "Heel" when I want to play the obedience game with him or when I want him to move to my side and sit. For loose-lead walking, including therapy dog visits, I say "By Me."

I used to work my dogs on lead tension. Now I believe keeping the leash loose is by far the best way to handle a dog. If you set your mind to it, you can change the tight leash habit in yourself and your dog in a week or two. Since a tight leash also increases a dog's defensiveness and we need a minimum of defensive attitude from a therapy dog, we have lots of reasons to train for a loose leash.

## TRAINING COLLARS

While teaching your dog to Heel on leash, you're making decisions about how to use the leash with your dog and what type of training collar to use. No one training collar is right for all dogs. Some trainers who are physically adept can work all dogs on the same type of collar, but they have skill most people lack.

The gentlest restraint on a dog is a harness around the shoulders and chest. A harness doesn't give you good control over the dog, unless you're much stronger than the dog. The harness takes pressure off the dog's throat, and I used it with miniature American Eskimo Angel, once she was trained. Harnesses are often appropriate for very small dogs.

The next step up is a buckle, or other nonslip collar, which every dog needs for its identification tags. Take it off only when the dog is in a crate or other situation where the collar could be a hazard. Some dogs can be trained on a buckle collar. It will at least give you control around the house.

Slightly more forceful are the various limited-slip collars. Some are designed to work from either side, an advantage with a beginning dog not yet used to working on your left. These collars must be fitted carefully, both for the fully tight fit and for the loose fit.

The slip collar made of chain, fabric or leather is the most traditional training collar, and works properly from only one direction. Form the collar into a loop by holding one ring in your left hand and other in your right hand. Feed the length of the collar down through the left ring for the letter P. Have a dog trainer or other knowledgeable person show you how to put the collar on and how to use it properly so that it will not choke the dog. A nylon snap-around collar can work well for some dogs in training. It snaps together rather than slipping over the dog's head, so it fits precisely.

If you use a slip collar on visits, stay alert for people sliding hands under the collar when it's loose, since tightening it could theoretically hurt them. I have never heard of such an injury actually occurring. A slip collar can serve as a safety precaution if your dog's head is smaller than the neck, as is true with several breeds. In case of a frightening episode such as a stray dog attacking in the parking lot, a buckle collar could slip over the dog's head. A slip collar is less likely to leave a dog both terrified and loose.

The prong collar (also called a pinch collar) exerts several times more force than a slip collar. It should be used only when a dog has little body sensitivity, and never on an aggressive dog, because it can increase defensiveness. The prong collar isn't harmful when used correctly, but is not suitable for therapy dog visits. If you feel you cannot adequately control your dog's exuberance

*The head halter is an effective and humane training collar--not a muzzle as people sometimes mistakenly think.*

without a pinch collar, work to develop in both your dog and yourself the constant habit of maintaining a loose lead. You will be pleasantly surprised at the difference when you master this skill.

Head halters have an extraordinary ability to give the handler control over a dog's mouth, ideal for aggressive dogs. The head halter doesn't increase defensiveness. Head halters also help handlers who lack sufficient strength to restrain their dogs, and these halters control barking, lunging and scavenging when on leash. A head halter can be a perfect tool to work your dog through a problem, while you are teaching focused attention and other commands.

Humans have a tendency to escalate the force when training dogs. Don't be this kind of trainer. Use the minimum force and the gentlest equipment necessary. The equipment is only a tool for control, and does not motivate the dog. Your goal is to teach the dog to respond to you.

## STAND FOR PETTING

The next exercise needed for basic work is the Stand. This is a Stay, but the dog gets petted. Therapy dogs must also hold steady for petting in the Sit and Down positions, but the Stand is hardest.

The Stand is not a long Stay. One minute is long enough. Adding time to this exercise too quickly will make some dogs quit. In actual therapy dog work, you'll use the Stand in a relaxed manner. Seldom will it matter whether the dog moves its feet slightly, but teaching the dog to keep the feet still is useful training.

To introduce the Stand to a puppy, use treats. You can lure the pup into a standing position by pulling the treat out in front of the nose, and release the treat with a "Good Stand!" when the puppy is standing. Don't push for the pup to hold the feet steady until it's older.

Teach the Stand on signal and verbal command. Don't wrestle the dog into position, because you will confuse the dog. My signal for Stand is to hold my right hand in front of the dog's nose, palm flat and toward the dog, with fingers spread apart. On Stand, as on Stay, the dog learns more easily if you teach the signal when the dog first learns the verbal command. Give command and signal at the same time.

*Here Bill has hooked his right thumb through Star's collar with his hand supporting her chin. His left hand is palm down, gently bracing her hind leg into a Stand.*

*Make sure the dog can Sit and Down for
petting before you try the Stand for petting.*

You can help your dog into a Stand by hooking your right thumb through the collar with your right hand under the chin as for the Sit, and holding your left hand, palm flat and facing down, against the front of the dog's right hind leg where it meets the body. The palm facing down helps keep you from poking the dog in the tummy, which will not help the training! Your hand in front of the leg locks it into position and prevents the dog from sitting or lying down. Get your hands away as quickly as possible.

I move forward one step with my left foot as I give the Stand signal. The dog has this space to stop, put its feet into a comfortable stance and Stand.

The Stand in obedience competition allows posing the dog, which is also useful when training a therapy dog. The most stable Stand position is with each leg vertical, not stretched out in a conformation show pose. Take the feet one at a time and move them into this position. Dogs react best if you first lightly touch the back and run your hand gently down the leg to the foot, rather than surprising the dog by grabbing the foot directly.

Introduce the petting portion of this exercise after the dog is steady. Before trying it, have someone pet your dog while it does Sit- and Down-Stays. Any difficulty with petting in these two positions indicates the dog is not ready for petting on the Stand. If the dog shows aggression when the person approaches, get expert help. The same applies if the dog runs away in panic from the person.

Both aggression and shyness come in degrees. Always have aggression evaluated, since it can become so dangerous. If the dog appears timid but can hold position and accept petting with no sign of aggression, just be sure to give it lots of social experience. In therapy dog work, some people respond wonderfully to a slightly timid dog, if the handler is able to give the dog proper support.

When your dog breaks the Stay to go wagging toward the petting person, don't give a harsh correction. This dog's heart is in the right place. Just practice faithfully and help the dog hold steady. Work on the Stand-Stay for awhile with only you petting the dog, and have people pet the dog when it is not on a Stay command. The dog may need to be older before its Stand will be reliable; some dogs mature late.

Don't rush the dog or use harsh corrections, because there is no substitute for adequate practice and maturity. You could ruin the dog. Handled correctly, the friendly, bouncy youngster may well have a longer working life than a less energetic dog, so you'll be ahead in the long run. Keep practicing, and appreciate your dog's good qualities.

## GREETING

The therapy dog needs to learn to greet people it will encounter in therapy work. I tell my dog, "Go say 'Hi'!" You can use any phrase you like, but it makes sense to include "go," which is used in commands to send the dog away from you.

I consider the Greeting a skill the therapy dog needs to master. It is not technically a command. The therapy dog should have some say in whether or not it wants to interact with a particular person. I don't believe in forcing a dog to give love.

*The Greeting is a special therapy dog skill. Timid dogs gain confidence from making the approach rather than having people bear down on them, while super-friendly dogs benefit from learning to wait for permission before approaching another person when out working with you.*

When training, I may occasionally insist, when I absolutely know the person won't hurt or scare my dog, but with strangers I give the dog a vote.

On the Greeting cue, the dog moves toward the person you indicate with a hand gesture. For a timid dog, this lets the dog go up to the person instead of the person coming to the dog. Timid dogs find it less stressful to make the approach themselves rather than have people bear down on them.

If your dog is reluctant to approach others, you can hand the person a treat to give your dog. Avoid treats if your dog snaps at fingers. The dog will feel less nervous if the person squats or kneels, and may feel more nervous if the person bends over its head. Over time, you will need to develop your dog's tolerance for a person bending over it and hugging, but take it slowly.

If you find that your puppy or dog still doesn't want to go up to the now-squatting person with the food, quickly abandon that approach. Start working your dog around people using the Attention exercise while having the people ignore your dog or puppy. This will allow your dog to get used to the situation more gradually, without being overloaded, and could very well save your dog's temperament.

With a boisterously friendly dog, the greeting teaches the dog not to approach people without permission. Don't jerk the dog back, just bring the dog's attention back to you with its name and your movement, or a different command, such as Sit. "Go say 'Hi'!" becomes the release giving a friendly dog permission to go greet the person. This control is necessary, because some people are afraid of dogs, allergic to them, or on their way to an important appointment in clothes they can't have decorated with dog hair!

For Believer, who dearly loved to jump up on people, I started using a new cue: "Cuddle." "Come Cuddle" tells her to come to my hands held at the level of my knees, for petting. "Go Cuddle" tells her to do it with another person. "Good Cuddle!" is a great way to praise her when she aims that love to the right spot, and doesn't try to jump up on the person.

Do not allow your therapy dog to jump up on people in greeting. The only exception is when you cue the dog to put paws on you, on your command. Lots of people will try to get your dog to jump up on them. Be polite, but be firm that your dog is not allowed to do that.

Start the no-jumping rule from the minute you get a puppy, or dog. Don't let anyone pet your puppy when it's standing on hind legs. Dogs don't jump on people to annoy them. They jump on people because PEOPLE have taught them this is the way to get close to loving hands and kissing faces, for affection. To teach your puppy or dog otherwise, start right now to give liberal affection when four feet are on the ground, and withhold affection from a dog standing on hind legs. Then you will never be tempted to do awful things to your dog such as stepping on its delicate toes, or shoving your knee into its ribcage, in a misguided attempt to stop the jumping up that you encouraged in the first place!

# 7

# SOCIAL SKILLS

This chapter is entitled "Social Skills," rather than "Socialization," because therapy dogs work by interacting with people. Socialization equips dogs to calmly tolerate various settings, such as the facility atmosphere. Therapy dogs interact and communicate with humans, requiring social skills beyond the basic ability to tolerate a situation.

Assistance dogs for people with disabilities are trained in public, because they must work in real situations in order to learn. Dogs know the difference between real life and set-up situations. Like assistance dogs, therapy dogs work in a variety of settings designed more for humans than for dogs. In training class, dogs and handlers learn commands, develop reliable control, and work on special problems. After that, work in the real world allows them to finish mastering social skills.

Dogs quickly detect emotional, mental and physical differences in humans. Unsocialized dogs can react negatively. Therapy dogs have consistently shown special understanding and tolerance. This positive response is developed through careful handler effort.

Dogs forgive accidents and actions by confused humans, if they believe their handlers and the facility staff will prevent such incidents from going too far. If you don't protect your dog, frightening or painful experiences will cause it to lose trust in the people and settings involved in therapy dog work. It might take a month, or it might take two years, but the breakdown of trust in a dog not adequately protected by its handler on therapy dog visits is only a matter of time.

## BE IN CONTROL: SAFETY IN PUBLIC

*Angel received valuable social experience when a neighborhood office supply store kindly allowed her to accompany me on regular shopping trips. I carried a notebook to spread in the bottom of the shopping cart for her comfortable footing.*

Before taking a dog out into challenging and sensitive public situations to work on social skills, you need enough control to ensure other people's safety around your dog at all times. Taking the dog out before this control is established risks both legal trouble and a dog ruined for later therapy dog work.

One way to test yourself is to work your dog on its commands and keep score. Leave your dog on a Sit-Stay, walk 30 feet away, and call the dog. The dog should come on one command at least eight or nine times out of ten before you begin to consider training reliable. Anytime the dog fails to come, it should come on the second command, without going out of control in any way.

If your dog is this steady on the command in varied settings, it has learned the exercise, though you must never stop training for improved control in the face of greater distractions. Go through a similar scoring process on all the basic control exercises. Work under conditions similar to the distractions you expect in the places you want to take your dog.

Such testing should not take place in one massive session. You might do two or three repetitions in a practice session, but ten at a time could depress your dog. Instead, look at responses in practice sessions for a week or two. Does the dog consistently obey each command? When the dog misses a command, does it ever go out of control?

Consider temperament before working the dog in public, too. If you've trained your dog in the basics, you've had the chance to observe it in many situations. How does it act at the veterinarian's office? Does it react negatively under any circumstances against children or men? Does it growl or lunge at other dogs? If your dog reacts aggressively toward any types of people or other dogs, have a qualified trainer help you evaluate the dog's temperament and your level of control as a team.

Some dogs simply aren't suited for therapy dog work. Others need lots of training first, perhaps more than you want to give. If you have doubts, even "funny feelings" you can't put into words, get help. A person's relationship with a dog is largely nonverbal. You may know something about your dog through this language without words.

Always keep in mind the limits of your dog's control. No matter how advanced, every dog has limits. Don't relax your attention as a handler when in public.

A young puppy is an exception to the rule of good control training, provided the puppy isn't aggressive or out of control. Take your puppy into every pleasant situation you possibly can. Follow your veterinarian's advice about where to take the pup to socialize with other dogs, until vaccinations are complete at twelve and a half weeks or so. But get the puppy out around all kinds of people and places for positive experiences during this very critical socialization period.

## BE IN CONTROL: SAFETY FOR THE DOG

*Since our home has no steps, we practice steps occasionally at a nearby building. A good routine for working on steps is to walk up the steps with the dog, have the dog Stay at the top, then call the dog down the steps to you.*

Just as important as ensuring the safety of others is protecting your dog at all times. Many dog owners fail in this, and ruin good therapy dogs. When the owner doesn't control a dog's experiences, the dog can develop bad attitudes and behaviors. Every experience influences a dog's future beliefs and reactions. The dog can't tell you what has happened; you have to know. This essential part of handling a therapy dog makes it a twenty-four-hour-a-day responsibility.

Control over the dog's environment begins at home. Make sure no one ever abuses the dog. Prevent the dog from having any opportunities to kill or injure other animals. These experiences can keep your dog from becoming a therapy dog.

Don't allow people around your dog who are drinking alcohol or using recreational drugs; it makes people's behavior too erratic. Don't leave the dog alone with young children. A child isn't mentally capable of empathy until between five and seven years of age. Even normal children under this age will mistreat dogs, especially when no adult is watching. The dog can then bite and develop a distrust of children. This is unfair to both the child and the dog.

The dog shouldn't be put at the mercy of anyone you can't totally trust to treat the dog well. You don't want a therapy dog to feel it must defend itself from people; you want it to look to you to protect it and to trust you. You achieve this by consistently and faithfully protecting your dog. Inappropriate handling at a grooming shop, a veterinarian's office or an obedience class can ruin a potential therapy dog.

## ALL TYPES OF PEOPLE AND SITUATIONS

Your goal is to work your dog around all the people and situations you might expect to encounter in therapy dog work or in your normal lifestyle with your dog. At the same time, you don't want to create or reinforce your dog in any fears.

*I bought this shopping cart at a moving sale. It was ideal for teaching Star to walk alongside a wheeled conveyance, and then giving her experience riding in it.*

Seek experiences with people of all races, people wearing unusual costumes, men with varying degress of facial hair, children, and anyone else you know to be harmless. Give everyone the same respect, and your dog will learn to do so as well. Help your dog learn to be comfortable with differences in people.

I teach my dogs on our outings to ignore inappropriate commands given by other people. If someone passing by or petting the dog gives it a command, I simply don't follow through on that command. If necessary, I give the dog a conflicting command. The dog must know to obey the handler, not just anyone in the area. Therapy dogs will have people on visits shouting inappropriate commands at them on occasion. I don't want my dog to worry about those commands at all.

I teach my dogs to interact socially with other people, but to take their commands from me. This relieves the dogs of having to determine who is in charge, who they must please, and how to interpret the commands of various handlers. They feel less stress interacting with strangers when they know I remain in charge. This kind of leadership from a handler gives certain types of dogs a deeper sense of security. If your dog would be comfortable taking commands from various handlers, you can train for this and use it in some types of therapy dog visits. Make a careful choice about how to handle your dog and then be consistent.

Whenever you see an unusual but safe situation, use it to educate your dog. For example, one morning out walking with Star, I came to a wooden stage set up for an outdoor performance in front of a neighborhood business. With the manager's permission, Star and I walked on it and I called her across it until she relaxed on the strange footing. The manager jokingly answered my request for permission by saying it was fine, as long as she didn't relieve herself on it. When I whipped out the plastic bags in my pocket with a smile and told him I was prepared to pick up, in the unlikely event of her having an accident, his eyes got huge! Later I was delighted to hear him telling other merchants. When people learn you will treat their property with respect, they give you more access to places for training!

In accustoming your dog to new situations, use your commands. Guide, support and help your dog by telling it what you want. Let the dog discover, through repeated experiences, that obeying you leads to success in every situation. This encourages the dog to look to you whenever in doubt, an excellent attitude for a therapy dog.

Working your dog on commands in public and in new situations lets you further develop the give-and-take between you and your dog. This is also your chance to develop the dog's initiative. You want this dog to become your partner and to tell you things you can't perceive with human senses. Communication often requires the dog to persist before you will understand. To encourage this in your dog, try hard to read what it is trying to tell you and never punish it for any effort to communicate with you.

Working in public will involve situations when the dog sees a hazard before you do, and the dog must disobey a command. If the dog makes an especially clever judgment call, be sure to praise the dog. Once I was walking with Star and stepped out from behind a parked van onto a lightly traveled road. Before I could see the on-coming car, Star had pulled me back from it. She got lots of praise!

Another time, I had Saint, Angel and Star on a Stay at a spot where the sidewalk jutted into a parking lot, when a big truck drove to the edge on its way around. The dogs moved. They were right—the truck could have easily rolled over the curb and hit them. I had them repeat the Stay, but not so near the edge. That's give-and-take, with the handler keeping control.

When your dog messes up a command, you should generally require it to repeat the exercise in exactly the same situation. In other words, put it exactly where it was in the first place for a Stay if it moved. In a case where the place from which the dog moved was unsafe, your moving the dog acknowledges your dog was correct to show you the problem. Having the dog repeat the exercise in the new spot is a good precaution against accidentally encouraging the dog to ignore your commands.

Be considerate of your dog. If you take a cold-sensitive dog out to practice Stays on a cold day, put a coat on the dog before asking it to Down for five minutes on icy pavement. Therapy dogs don't have to be able to work in ice-cold conditions, after all! On hot days, work only on pavement that's been in the shade for hours. The dog will try harder to please you when your commands are consistently reasonable. At the same time, everyone who sees you training will feel good about your treatment of the dog. This makes your work far more acceptable in public.

Look at things from the dog's perspective. Once I asked Saint to jump into an obstacle on a playground. He kept refusing, while I kept insisting. He finally did it, and I saw what he'd realized all along: it was too narrow inside for him to land. I guess I expected him to do a handstand! I apologized to him. Dogs understand when you admit you were wrong. When you treat them more considerately the next time, they learn to trust you.

The handling skills you develop working your dog in public will carry over to therapy dog visits. You need to know what your dog is thinking. It's not easy, but spending the training time and learning the give-and-take with your dog will make it happen.

Be ready to drop down and get your eyes to the dog's eye level to see what it sees. Watch your dog carefully, and constantly. Since dogs use body language instead of words, time spent watching the dog is the equivalent of time spent listening to a human. Watch your dog interact with other dogs and other people. When you are watching and not involved with the interaction, you can learn things you would never learn any other way.

In training classes and competitive events, the "world" is structured and controlled. In the real world, you and your dog will develop skills for therapy dog visits impossible to learn in structured settings. You need the structure first. Then get out and apply the skills in real life.

## LEARN TO "READ" PEOPLE

One of the basic skills you'll work on when out with your dog is the ability to "read" people. You and your dog both need this skill. It's a complex task of interpreting people's body language as well as their words.

Watch people closely and listen to them carefully. At first, don't let your dog go near anyone unless the person asks. As you gain skill, you can sometimes give the dog the greeting cue when the person has indicated he or she wants to be near the dog but hasn't actually asked. You'll learn to respond to things like the person reaching a hand toward the dog, or looking at the dog in a longing way. When you aren't sure, ask the person if he or she likes dogs. If you make a wrong decision and take the dog near people who don't want you to, you'll learn to read this in their faces and body language. Then, of course, calmly move your dog away.

You don't need to jump into working on social skills all at once. You can start taking your dog out on walks in places that are not crowded, to practice basic control work, and teach the dog to work around people. Practicing basic commands in public is important throughout the dog's career. As you work with the dog, people will naturally be interested, and social interaction will develop. Remember never to correct the dog when it's in the act of being friendly.

*Placing the dog in a Down-Stay while you smile at people soon puts them at ease.*

## COURTESY IN PUBLIC

In public you'll observe people showing various emotions when they see your dog. Just as a dog learns to guide a blind person by bumping the trainer into things, you'll learn by observing and responding to these emotions. Courtesy in public includes not only such things as picking up feces if your dog has an accident but extreme consideration for other people in every way. If you take the dog to relieve itself in an acceptable place before and after each outing to avoid your dog marking the whole neighborhood and then feeling led to guard the territory it has marked, this rarely will happen.

Saint was invited into a neighborhood shoe store to practice his social skills.

If this seems unreasonable, remember you're practicing to work with people who can't always tell you how they feel, and who may have no choice about being around your dog when you enter the facility. Learn good skills by working with people who can tell you if you're bothering them. The more you learn to read people's expressions and respond instantly to their feelings, the more you will develop as a therapy dog handler.

When you smile toward people's faces, observe their expressions. If they look nervous about the dog, don't approach any nearer. I routinely stop when walking a large dog in my neighborhood shopping center and have the dog Sit-Stay or Down-Stay until any nervous-looking person has passed. If you were going to the grocery store or to buy a pair of shoes and were afraid of dogs, and there was a big one right in your path, perhaps coming right at you, how would you feel? What if the handler gave you a friendly smile and had the dog lie down well out of your way until you got into the store or to your car? What if you were an older person and unsure of your footing? You might like dogs but you don't know this one. It could cause you to fall on this hard pavement. How would you feel?

What if you were a mom or dad carrying a baby or a grandparent with your grandchild, perhaps shepherding one or two other young children while they run ahead and explore? You know those young'uns are going to run up and touch the dog, and you don't know anything about this dog or its owner. If handler and dog show you friendly, steady control and concern for your needs and feelings, would you mind the dog being there? Probably not.

Working your dog around the public means reaching out to other people and learning to control the situation. This skill will be exactly the same when you start working in facilities with your dog.

The way your dog looks will make your job more or less difficult. It took me years to learn how to put people at ease around Saint, with his large, black, short-haired, erect-eared body. On the other hand, it was rare to find anyone afraid of small, white, fluffy Angel. Gabriel and Believer, large, but fluffy and smiling, win friends quickly.

Until you can put everyone at ease around your dog, don't try therapy dog visits. You'll have to master other handling skills in order to master this one. It requires handler and dog to have good control work, social ability, and the rapport to work with positive handling no matter what the situation. People have every right not to have to feel afraid.

## PUT PEOPLE AT EASE

As you move from practicing with your dog in private to working in public, your control work will be the means of putting people at ease around your dog. Ironically, a large dog obedient to commands not only relaxes well-meaning people who

*My neighbors the Amyxes invited Gabriel into their home and helped us practice with their active young boys.*

fear dogs, but also inspires the respect of bad guys! If the dog obeys you, they assume it will protect you, too. You won't get sued when out with your leashed, large, obedient, friendly dog, yet you'll have all the protection you're ever likely to need.

After control, the next most important element in putting people at ease around your dog is for you to smile at them. If a sinister-looking person is following you and you don't want to invite him or her closer, don't look at the person. Leave doubt about your attitude and discourage interaction by giving no expression. But when you meet a nonthreatening person when out with your dog, a smile builds a bridge of goodwill.

Why is it so important for you to smile? First, people instinctively know your dog will probably back up your attitude. Trained or not, dogs tend to behave as their owners encourage them to behave.

Second, when I smile at a person while working my dog, I express confidence in my control over the dog. A smile combined with obvious control encourages people to trust a handler. Be sure to exercise control over your dog, though. A smiling handler with an out-of-control dog looks like an unreliable idiot!

Why take the time and trouble to be nice to people you meet in public when training a therapy dog? If you're in a public place, people in charge can either ask you to leave, or make a new rule: "No dogs allowed." It happens all the time, all over the world, mostly because of inconsiderate dog owners. Therapy dog handlers need to be just the opposite. In the process, you'll win friends for dogs, as well as access to more places to practice with your therapy dog.

Earning the access you need for effective therapy dog training requires you to earn your community's trust. If you find yourself unwelcome in public with your dog, it's time to take a hard look at your skills.

Generally, people with purposes unrelated to our dogs are the ones who pay the expenses for building and maintaining public places. Handlers who wish to be welcome there with dogs must respect the purpose of each place. If it's a business, for example, handlers who interfere with customers or employees trying to conduct business will be asked to leave.

When out practicing, you will encounter people who can benefit from the therapy dog. Taking time for them is a service to your community, as well as the best practice you will find.

## TRAINING IN PUBLIC

If you've learned to give gruff commands to your dog, you will need to learn a new style of handling for working your dog in public and for therapy dog work. It has traditionally been standard practice in dog training to use a firm command tone. On group Stays in the obedience ring, I always had to wait for other handlers to finish commanding their dogs in thundering tones before it was quiet enough to give my dog our pleasant-voiced command.

I trained my dogs to a pleasant voice because my goal, before therapy dog work even entered the picture, was to walk with them in my neighborhood. I didn't want to roar commands in the street, especially when walking in early morning or after dark. I wanted my dogs to obey polite commands and handling.

*The sidewalk in front of stores in a strip shopping center is an ideal place to work on therapy dog social skills. Wait until you and your dog are really ready, though, or merchants will ask you to leave and you'll lose a valuable training location for the future.*

The way you handle your dog will determine people's opinions of you and your dog. If you treat the dog with obvious love and respect, people will think more highly of you both, trust you, and accept your presence more willingly in public places.

Also, people tend to treat your dog the way you treat it. Your kindness toward the dog becomes a model for them. I've seen this many times, but one occasion took me by surprise. A nursing-home resident had invited Angel to stand on hind legs for petting. When she finished petting Angel, the lady gently lowered her front legs to the ground, just as I do for my dogs. It reduces joint stress and the risk of arthritis as the dog ages. This loving action deeply touched me.

Principles for training in public:

1. Address your dog in a pleasant voice. Don't use a "mean" tone.
2. Make corrections brief. Come out praising the next instant.
3. Don't use "lay in wait" tactics when training in public.

Instead, work closely with the dog and teach it not to start the misbehavior. For example, don't let your dog lunge at—and possibly traumatize—another person or dog so you can correct it.

4. Don't go into a shop and leave the dog out of your sight on a Stay outside. It's not fair to the dog, to other people or to their dogs. Stay where you can see your dog. Don't step away from the dog on Stays in public unless you know the dog is reliable. Don't do it in a situation that's going to make customers nervous, either.

5. Praise at least ten times as much as you correct, and say it like you mean it.

6. When in public, work on things the dog does well and enjoys. Concentrate on teaching the dog what you want, rather than what you don't want.

7. Beware of burnout. Find sources of inspiration, and continually work to improve your skills. Don't work the dog, especially in public, when you can't muster up a happy mood and a positive attitude.

8. Take time to talk to people who approach you with questions. Consider this your "rent" for training in public places. Train in private on days you don't have time for people.

9. Read books about assistance dog training. These trainers work regularly in public, too, and like therapy dog handlers, they train dogs for the real world. The main difference is that therapy dogs interact with other people, while guide dogs learn to ignore other people when working.

10. Listen to comments people make when watching you with your dog in public, especially those they don't mean for you to hear. Some are nonsense, but sometimes people see things you don't see. Often it will be inappropriate for you to say anything, but food for thought later. A good trainer is always evaluating him- or herself, admitting mistakes and working to improve. It's far too easy to form the habit of blaming the dog, or blaming other people.

# 8

# EXTRA CONTROL WORK AND HAND SIGNALS

Your dog's temperament and your handling skills will determine how early in the training process you can safely work in public. All my dogs did much of their basic training on the streets in the neighborhood. Some owners and dogs will need to learn all the basic command work first. Every new command you and your dog master together is another option for control.

*Working the dog in a chair with wheels can give the two of you an additional skill for therapy dog visits. Remember never to move the chair abruptly with the dog in it.*

Learning new skills will keep work lively and interesting for both you and the dog. Previous work will improve as you add new knowledge. You will be able to help people more fully on therapy dog visits. Your relationship with your dog will deepen, and the two of you will become a more effective team.

Dogs, handlers and facilities are all different, with different needs. Beyond basic control work, customize the training to your situation. In life, you can't remain in one place; you're always either moving forward or moving backward. This is certainly true of dog training skill, for both dog and handler. I hope the ideas here will move you forward, and inspire you to keep progressing for as long as you work with therapy dogs.

## TRAINING SIGNALS

Commands given by signal are extremely useful in therapy dog work. Signals help when your dog cannot, for whatever reason, hear you. Signals let you cue the dog without speaking, to preserve the atmosphere in a particular situation. And adding a signal to a verbal command adds emphasis to the dog, allowing you to "insist" on the command without resorting to an unpleasant voice.

As a beginning dog trainer, I remember poring over pictures in dog books and asking other trainers for signals to teach my dogs. As they told me, anything you want can be a signal, but I often tried several different signals before finding the one my dog responded to best. So I'll give you my signals, to get you started. Feel free to make up your own, or borrow from others. As with tone of voice, experiment with your signals to learn what communicates best for your dog.

### Sit

I have two signals for Sit, one for close, the other for distance. When the dog is near me, I use the right hand, palm upward, fingers extended and together. My wrist may remain straight to use the entire forearm, or I may just bend the wrist if I'm right in front of

*Sit signal, for close situations such as those most common in therapy dog settings.*

the dog's nose. I bring my hand straight up, briskly.

The farther and faster the hand travels, the more emphatic the signal. As you and your dog progress, you'll use less movement, and when you use a bigger signal, your dog will respond the same way as to the difference between a soft voice and a louder voice on a verbal command. This aids control when your dog is distracted.

For my Sit signal from a distance, I use the left arm. The palm faces the dog to start, and the hand travels to the front, rotates to the highest point over my head and backwards to my side through a continuous circle. So, it starts at my side and circles front, up, back and down to my side. Make the movement as fast as you can, because dogs see movement much better than they see a motionless object.

*Sit signal for distance. You might use this for demonstrations, and it helps your dog learn to focus on you.*

On actual therapy dog visits you need to get the dog's attention before giving a signal, since the dog's work involves looking at other people rather than always at you. The dog can learn to give you attention on its name, at the snap of your fingers, clap of your hands, slap on your thigh, scrape of your foot on the floor, or any number of other sounds. You can also wave a hand to catch the dog's eye, or lightly touch the dog.

Avoid moving your shoulders, head or other part of your body when teaching your dog a hand signal. These movements will become part of your signal to your dog, unbeknownst to you! A mirror or store window can help you check yourself. You may never use the signals at a distance on a therapy dog visit, but teaching them will intensify your dog's ability to focus and respond to you.

### Down

My Down signal also depends on the dog's distance from me. The Down signal is given with the palm downward. To Down a dog beside me, I use the first two fingers. I lean over, hold the extended first two fingers of my right hand in front of the dog's nose, and draw the fingers to the floor for the dog's nose to follow as the dog goes Down.

This is a clear and gentle signal to elicit obedience from a cooperative dog. I saw the power of this signal at an obedience event when another handler asked me how she could get her dog to Down in the ring. He was refusing to Down right then in practice. I showed her my signal, and minutes later in the ring, her dog, new to this signal, obeyed it!

*Down signal for distance.*

My Down signal from a distance is similar to the Sit. I use the right arm for the Down, because I first teach the signals at a distance in the same order: Down, Sit, then Come. Alternating arms—always using the right arm for Down, the left for Sit, and the right for Come—lets my dog learn the signals easily. Later I vary the order and use the signals in other situations to broaden the dog's training. Like the Sit, the Down signal starts at my side, this time with the palm facing away from the dog. I rotate the arm back, up, front and down to my side.

I especially like these signals because, unlike signals such as raising one arm, I don't move my arm through a full rotation by accident when working my dog. If I straighten my glasses or hair, it won't look to my dog like a signal. The full rotation of my arm also seems clearer to the dog, and provides physical therapy for my arthritis!

When the dog already knows a command word, you can teach a signal by first giving the signal, then saying the word. With repetitition, the dog starts to expect the word after the signal, and begins to respond to the signal in anticipation of the verbal command. Then you can drop the word.

When the dog doesn't see or fails to obey the signal, you can use the word as a mild correction. Say "no-o," or another sound, such as "Uh-oh!" when the dog misses the signal. Then say the command word, a repeat of the signal, or both together. A strong correction is to walk to the dog and put its body through the motion of the command. You need not be rough to make this a powerful correction. Start signal training close to the dog, so you can promptly position the dog whenever it fails to respond, and to avoid the fault of the dog creeping forward.

I like to train until the dog will watch me for up to fifteen seconds between signals. Be sure to vary the intervals to keep the dog flexible. Dogs have an acute sense of time and will sometimes learn to perform an action at a specific time interval, even without a command, unless you vary the number of seconds between commands to avoid setting such a pattern.

You don't want the dog to anticipate and change to the next position without your signal. Whenever the dog makes this mistake, mildly say "no," put the dog back into the previous position, and have it wait for your signal. Sometimes give a different signal than your dog expects, or give the Release. I like to condition my dogs to come to me for petting on the Release, as a safety feature and an additional reward. Build distance on signals gradually, working up to about sixty feet. As your dog ages, signals can help you check its eyesight. This is valuable information with the aging therapy dog.

## Heel

You can also teach your dog a signal for Heel. Dogs learn to take as a signal the movement of your left foot, if you always step out with the left foot after the Heel command. If you want to pattern the dog this way, start on the right foot whenever you leave the dog to Stay.

For my Heel signal, I turn the palm of my left hand toward my leg, hold the fingers straight and together, and move the hand forward, then back to my side. Giving this signal sometimes with the dog starting from several feet behind you helps teach Heel position.

## Come

Most handlers use the same signal for Come. It's given with the right arm, although like most signals, the dog will understand it almost as easily if for some reason you have to change arms. From base position hanging vertically at your side, raise and extend your right arm horizontally to your side, level with your shoulder, palm toward the dog. Without pausing, bring the hand sharply across your chest, palm inward now, in a beckoning motion. Then drop it back down at your side.

*Come signal.*

Considering all the places you will go with your therapy dog for training and visits, the Come signal is an important safety measure. You might find yourself in a situation with so much noise that the dog can't hear your voice. If you've been doing attention exercises and signals with your dog, the dog will naturally turn eyes to check on you frequently, and you can save the situation with this signal.

## Go Out, Take It, Go Say "Hi!"

To send my dog forward from me (Go Out), I gesture with the right hand, first two fingers extended, moving my hand from the dog's head forward. The signal for the retrieve can be the same, or you can use the left arm shooting forward from your side.

*Go Out, Take It, or Go Say "Hi" signal, depending on the accompanying verbal command.*

*This signal gives the dog a clear line to an object for retrieving.*

A stationary signal, to give your dog a precise line to a retrieve or to greet a specific person, is most clear if you hold your forearm and hand in a straight line above the dog's head (the palm of your hand vertical, not horizontal), just between its eyes. Try it on yourself, to see how a hand at the side of your head gives an unclear direction, and a hand above your head between your eyes points to the target precisely.

If the person I want the dog to greet is quite near, I've found dogs respond well to "waggling" fingers. I point my fingers toward the floor, extended and slightly spread, as I waggle them and move the hand from the dog's nose toward where I want the dog to focus. This signal also helps when a dog gets distracted.

### Paws Up

Another important signal and command for the therapy dog is Paws Up. This transfers to anything you want the dog to put front feet on; pat the object and say "Paws up."

I teach my dogs this as the only acceptable time and manner to jump on me. I hold my forearm out and have the dog put front feet there for a hug or kiss, as a reward. Paws Up is ideal for getting a therapy dog's paws to the arm of a wheelchair, a bedrail or the edge of a bed so a person with limited mobility can pet the dog. You can easily teach the dog the difference between Paws Up—just the front feet to the spot you pat—and Come Up, when you need the whole dog on the spot. If there is any doubt your dog might misinterpret the command, hold the

*The Paws Up command and signal brings the dog's feet to your forearm. You can tap on your inviting forearm with the other hand, or just use the extension of your forearm as the signal. Teach your therapy dog NOT to jump up on other people, even if they invite it, to minimize the risk of accidents. Give a conflicting command to your dog when someone cues it to jump up, and BIG praise to the dog for not jumping.*

*Sitting in the chair yourself is an excellent way to teach the dog to put paws on the arm for petting situations. This also works for bedrails. I prefer supporting the dog's forelegs myself, to protect the dog and the person's skin.*

collar when you give the Paws Up command. Then you can prevent the dog from leaping onto a bed inappropriately, and the dog's understanding will increase, too. For maximum control, have the dog do Paws Up to your forearm and then you place the paws in the desired spot.

## TREATS

People occasionally try to feed their medications and other harmful things to therapy dogs. If you want to allow treats, it's wise to bring them yourself. Remain alert to prevent your dog from eating anything else offered by another person. Inappropriate feeding jeopardizes the dog's health, safety, and training. Dogs can become incredibly distractible and difficult to handle around food on therapy dog visits if they are expecting to get some of it. They will also drool more, which you then have to mop up from slick floors.

Broken skin on a person from a dog's teeth, even when the dog intended no harm, can cause nasty and expensive consequences for dog and handler. Even if your dog is normally gentle when taking

*The safest way to give a dog a treat is from the palm of your hand—but it's sloppy!*

treats from humans, having people feed the dog on therapy dog visits is risky. I choose not to allow it with my dogs.

There are three somewhat safe ways to give a dog a treat. You can hold the treat in the palm of your hand. The hand will get slobbery, but the dog will probably take the treat gently, because snapping won't work. You can toss the treat to the dog. Restrain the dog on leash until the treat lands, so the dog won't lunge unpredictably to catch it, possibly injuring itself or someone else. You can put the dog on a Stay command, set the treat down and release the dog to take it. This has the effect of a trick rather than an interaction with a person, which can miss the point of the therapy dog visit.

If you plan to allow people to feed your therapy dog, train the dog to take food gently from fingers. Teach this by not releasing the treat until the dog takes it correctly, with its teeth not touching your skin. You should feel only soft lips and tongue. This training is an extra safety measure, but you can still have accidents with treats.

*To teach your dog not to put teeth on fingers when taking treats, clench your hand and refuse to release the treat until you feel only gentle lips and tongue.*

Besides accidents, treats can make people think therapy dogs only respond to people for food. Too many people already believe this. I prefer to work therapy dogs on their social instincts and let people see the dogs truly enjoying their work. The best therapy dogs will have strong social drives and a desire to please their handlers. They will interact with friendly strangers in partnership with their handlers. Food will not be necessary.

I started Believer with treats for focused attention, and phased out the treats after four or five months. As I began to work her

*Before allowing people on therapy dog visits to give your dog treats, the dog needs to be trained to take them from fingers. You may decide it's simply not worth the risk of the dog getting overly excited and grabby for food.*

part of the time without treats, I noticed that people were more interested in petting her when I did not use treats. One reason was that with my hands free, I was petting her more myself. This provides a model for other people to pet the dog, and is very powerful in many situations. The other thing different without treats was a decrease in Believer's intensity. She looks calmer and more approachable when she is not working for treats. This would surely vary from one dog to another.

Letting people give treats to the dog can be meaningful in certain therapeutic interactions. If you choose to allow it, condition your dog to take the food gently, and make sure the dog will also work without food. Monitor the situation constantly, because a dog hungrier than usual or a treat tastier than usual can make the dog grabbier than usual.

## GREETINGS: SHAKE HANDS, KISS, NOSE, HEAD ON LAP

Two extra skills your therapy dog can use to good advantage are greetings: shaking hands and kissing. These are in addition to the basic greeting where the dog approaches a person for petting. I don't recommend forcing a dog to learn either of these behaviors. Just encourage whatever natural inclination the dog shows, and use a word for the behavior. Over time, the dog will learn what you mean when you say "Shake hands" or "Kiss."

Shaking hands is a submissive gesture from the dog, so teach it gently. Support the paw without squeezing it, and don't grab the foot or hold it too long. Monitor other

*If your dog likes to shake hands and has a gentle style, many people will be delighted to make the acquaintance!*

people when your dog shakes hands with them, to protect the dog from harm. Gradually, through play, you can build your dog's tolerance for less-gentle handling of the feet, in case someone does latch on too hard.

*Sometimes a sweet dog kiss is the perfect touch.*

You can help a dog learn to shake hands by gently lifting the designated paw from behind while offering your other hand (or someone else's) in front to shake it.

Proceed cautiously with training, and watch for your dog's individual style. Some dogs will vigorously claw at people in the process of shaking hands. It's better not to have such dogs shake hands with other people at all, until you can systematically reduce the force of their response by gentle and consistent restraint.

At first I thought people wouldn't like therapy dogs to lick them, but I was wrong. Many people love it, and it stimulates them in positive ways. Therefore, I suggest you teach the dog when to stop licking by gently pulling the dog back when licking is not wanted. Direct any licking away from the person's mouth, since that could carry a very slight risk of disease transmission. When you want your dog to stop licking you, pull away, or hold the dog's head back gently with your hand. A rough correction might stop the dog from ever licking again.

An optional behavior you can encourage in your dog is to Nose a person's hand. Some dogs will learn this just for the petting, while with others you might need to use treats at first. If the dog gets too enthusiastic, someone's cup of juice can go flying, so take this one slowly.

Some dogs enjoy putting their heads on people's laps, a charming behavior you will certainly want to encourage. This would also be easy to teach with treats.

## WALKING SKILLS: WAIT, EASY, MOVE, BACK, SIDE, AND GO THROUGH

For walking in public as well as on visits, you will want to teach your dog some more advanced walking behaviors. These are also used in other dog jobs.

The first of these special commands is Wait, which tells the dog to stop. Some trainers use Wait for a Stay soon to be followed by a moving command, but I'm talking about something different here. If you use the word "Wait" for a competition command, you'll want to use a different word for this.

After stopping the dog with Wait, I allow it to change body position, as long as it stays in one spot. I want the dog to feel free to sit or lie down if we stop for a long time and it gets tired. This lets the dog relax while I talk to someone. If I do not want the dog to change body position, I use Stay instead of Wait. I like the word "wait" in this situation, because it does not sound discourteous if passing people think I'm talking to them!

A second walking cue is whether or not you want the dog to pull. If your dog pulls a racing sled or dog cart, you'll learn a specific command from that work. I say "Go-go!" with extra zest to encourage pulling.

When I want the dog to stop pulling but continue moving forward, I say "Easy." This word also works the dog through a situation in which you want it to move gently and carefully, and to take further cues from you. I use Easy to steer a dog through broken glass, or when coming down steps together. If you've ever had a dog pull you down a flight of steps, you'll appreciate this command!

"Move" means "heads up, you're in my way." I use this around the house and on walks frequently, and occasionally it helps on a therapy dog visit. You don't want your dog to panic and jump when you say this, so be gentle when you nudge your dog, or move it a step or two by the collar to teach it. Remember to say "Stay" when you do not want the dog to move, so you don't mix your signals and fall over the dog.

These days I frequently use the command Back. I have taught my dogs to step backwards at my side. A good way to introduce this is no more than about three steps at a time, with the dog between you and a wall. The dog may panic, so give enthusiastic encouragement and reward. Eventually it becomes an elegant way to remind the dog not to pull. When Gabriel's leash goes tight, I can stop and have him take backward steps with me. Look behind you before stepping backward, so you don't run into anything or anyone.

I often find on therapy dog visits or in other public settings that someone who must pass the dog in a tight place is nervous. Sometimes it's necessary for me to pass the person. For such occasions, I've taught Gabriel and Believer a command, "Side," which means for the dog to walk on my right instead of my left. Like the Back, Side is easy to teach a little at a time when you happen to be walking alongside a wall.

"Go Through" has become one of my favorite cues. I point ahead of the dog's nose as if for a greeting, but the words tell Gabriel I want him to move through an opening ahead of me. I use Go Through when passing through a narrow space in a hallway between people. I use it to send Gabriel under a bedside tray or walker to someone for petting. I even used it once to bring Star to me under a low coffee table, when psychiatric patients had her cornered between sofa and coffee table. Now Gabriel knows how to skinny under the coffee table, too!

## POSITIONS IN PLACE

Teach your large therapy dog positions-in-place, with words and signals for Sit, Down and Stand. When you meet someone who's afraid of your dog, don't crowd the person. Remaining in one spot, give your dog pleasant verbal commands and gentle but obvious signals for the positions. Praise each position response. Go through the set of three commands two times. This sequence relaxes people by showing your control and the dog's easy obedience.

Teach positions-in-place gently. It's a powerful exercise and can make a dog feel oppressed. Most commands need to have good reason, or you jeopardize the quality of initiative in your dog. Excessive drill destroys initiative. Practice positions-in-place just enough to instill good discipline, and season it liberally with praise.

## FRONT, FINISH

The Front position, dog and handler facing one another with the dog seated, is useful when lining your dog up beside or between wheelchairs for petting. It's easy to make a dog go sour on its work by teaching Fronts too harshly. Don't grab at the dog or use the leash to yank the dog into a straight Front. You want the dog to come to you happily. Encourage the position by backing up, and leaning back slightly with your upper body while encouraging your dog to your hands for petting. Treats and play rewards can strengthen the Front response. This is an easy exercise to teach while developing the Attention work.

*Front position helps line the dog up for petting. I've taught my dogs to "Come Through" between two wheelchairs to "Front."*

The Finish is a refinement of Heel position. To Finish, the dog starts in Front position, then comes to Heel either by tightly circling 180 degrees counterclockwise and

*This elegant method for teaching the around-behind finish is perfect for therapy dogs. Start by standing toe-to-toe with your dog.*

*Next, step first your right foot then your left foot up beside your dog, the two of you still facing opposite directions.*

*Raise your left arm and look under it, twisting your upper body as you encourage your dog to come on around you and sit at your left side. When I tried this method with little Angel, she learned the exercise rapidly.*

stopping seated at your left; or by going around your right side, behind you, and stopping seated at your left. For therapy dog purposes, teach these through your footwork, minimizing leash jerks or wild play incentives.

I teach my dogs both Finish directions, for maximum maneuverability on therapy dog visits. Though intended for the dog starting from Front, Finish exercises can bring a dog to Heel from ahead of you as well. I often have a dog Finish to correct a tight leash. It's one more way to both practice skills and keep the dog guessing as to what will come next, which is the key to loose leash walking.

Working on Finishes is useful polish and will improve your skill with the leash. If you have a large therapy dog, knowing both Finishes will help get your dog quickly out of the flow of traffic for people to pass. Sometimes you'll have room for the dog to move to your side from only one direction. There might be only enough room on your left for the dog to slip in after starting from your right. Or there might be no room on your right, only on your left.

The footwork for the Finish to your left starts by stepping back with your left foot. Guide the dog with your left hand holding the leash to teach the dog a signal with that hand. As the dog turns toward you (counterclockwise), step forward to your original position, helping the dog follow the movement of your left foot. With the progression of the training, you will take shorter steps, then none at all.

For the around-behind Finish, one method starts with the leash in your right hand, the foundation for a signal. Step back with your right foot, two steps for a large dog. Guide the dog around behind you (starting to your right), change the leash behind your back to your left hand, and step forward with your left foot as you guide the dog into a Sit in Heel position. Over time, reduce and then eliminate the foot movements.

An excellent alternative method for the around-behind Finish comes from dog trainer Michael Tucker. Starting with the dog in Front position, step forward and stand at your seated dog's right, the two of you facing opposite directions. Then twist your upper body left and backward to look under your raised left arm, and encourage the dog around you to Heel. Gradually move your feet less and less until the dog does all the traveling. The last stage before you stop moving your feet entirely can be just pointing your right toe toward a spot to the left of the dog's right foot. Two typical Finish commands are Heel and Swing, but feel free to make up your own. The dog doesn't care which one you use for which direction, as long as you are consistent.

When you and your dog have progressed on the two finish commands to the point of your not making any foot movements, start practicing with a wall behind you. This simulates one of the most common situations for using the Finish commands on therapy dog visits, which is to tuck yourself and your dog neatly against a wall to allow others to pass. The wall may bother your dog at first, so give extra encouragement.

## LANGUAGE

In everything you do with your dog, language plays a part. The more words your dog knows, the better. Teach new words as a natural part of relating to your dog.

Continuous verbal encouragement ("Good dog! You can do it!") can strongly motivate your dog and help your work. You can only use this technique if you accustom your dog to it. Otherwise your voice will distract the dog. Use a nickname for your dog with verbal encouragement, or no name, so the dog won't think you are giving a new command. Verbal encouragement helps keep a dog working on a command you have already given.

You can teach your dog commmands in a foreign language, or secret cues only you and the dog understand. Sometimes you may want to conceal your cues, for those people you'll visit who enjoy being with the dog with little involvement from you. I use subtle cues, including signals, to remain in control yet not intrude on the interaction.

Some competition handlers don't use the dog's name before any command. Others instruct students to use the name only when commanding the dog to move. The reasoning is to have the dog respond instantly when it hears its name, for the best score. The name is then not used with Stay commands.

I tend to use the dog's name with any command, for two reasons. I talk to my dogs a lot and frequently use verbal encouragement. In order for this not to be a distraction, and so the dog can distinguish a command from other talk, I preface every command with the dog's name. This is also important on therapy dog visits, when I'm talking to the people while also handling my dog. My dogs are together except when I take one out to work. In order to have good control of a pack of dogs, I need to say which dog I'm commanding. By using names with commands, I can command different dogs to do different things.

Another reason for using the dog's name with a command is something I did intuitively before I realized why. When I want the dog to perform a command action, but not as a command, such as on the veterinarian's examining table, I use the name after the command word. This is a weaker form of addressing the dog, which is why we normally use the dog's name before any command: "Gabriel, Come!" not "Come, Gabriel!" Gabriel alerts to his name and responds more accurately if the name comes first—he's more likely to hear the command word.

Therefore, when I want to give the dog some latitude about the command word, I don't use the command name first. I change my voice tone, and I physically assist the dog in the action. I may also add extra words to the command ("Star, can you Sit?"), or repeat it like a chant. This is the handling I want on the veterinarian's table and in stressful moments during a therapy dog visit. If the situation suddenly becomes critical, I give a command briskly. Such moments are why we teach commands as just those few words, not repetition, not extra signals or coaxing. A command is a command, the first time you say it, if you use your command voice and language consistently. Dogs easily learn these differences.

Make it a habit to use positive language with your dog. This will give you a more positive attitude toward the dog and will make the right impression when working your dog in public. A positive name for your dog is also important, and positive nicknames: Handsome, not Ugly. Clever Girl, not Dumb Dog.

Experiment with ways to get your dog to try new things. Use your voice and body language to see if you can communicate unusual actions to your dog. You might have your dog Stand on the sofa, for example, or Sit on the cool hood of your car. These are fun learning experiences for both of you. Do these activities in a spirit of play, and don't correct the dog for failing to understand. By rewarding the dog for trying, you build in your dog the important quality of persisting in a task. At the same time, you expand your handling skills and your dog's sophistication.

To get a fast response from your dog, say a command quickly but clearly, and the same way every time. It doesn't need to be loud, but rather short and clipped, or "staccato." Another musical term helpful for dog training is "dynamics"—varying the volume to vary the meaning. Musical people make good dog trainers.

You can use tones to "orient" your dog. As we discussed under corrections in the Conditioning to Handling chapter, you can teach your dog a sound like "Aaaaaa!" to stop what it's doing and look to you for instructions. This sound comes from your gut, forced sharply out by your diaphragm.

## DOES YOUR THERAPY DOG NEED A HOBBY?

Some dogs have so much energy, they're unlikely to make good house dogs without an outlet. Some high-energy dogs need time to mature, perhaps even several years, before developing the necessary composure for therapy dog work. These dogs need activities. People we visit enjoy all kinds of dogs, and if the dogs have had colorful careers, all the better.

Most of the activities people pursue passionately with their dogs can also be done casually, for fun, without interfering with therapy dog visits. If you choose this route, make sure the instructor and other participants understand and support your priorities.

## TRICKS

Whether your therapy dog performs tricks is up to you. Tricks taught with a playful attitude are fun and easy. Many tricks encourage useful skills, and entertainment can be therapeutic. A therapy dog visit consists primarily of interaction between the dog and people. Handlers who enjoy entertaining with their dogs need to be careful never to discourage other therapy dog handlers from visiting without performing.

What tricks can you use? You might be surprised at what becomes a trick if the dog will perform on cue and under control. Catching, fetching, demonstrating basic obedience exercises, and controlled games with your dog can all work. Not every dog has the instincts or physique for every trick. The fewer and lighter your props, the better. Many surfaces in health-care facilities are unsafe for jumping.

A good therapy dog team watches for people moving around when performing on a visit, to avoid running into anyone. The showy, "fired from a gun" response so desirable in competition is dangerous in a nursing home or other facility, unless the performance area can be kept absolutely clear of people. The quick response you value in competition will deteriorate over time, too, if used in inappropriate situations.

The dog will make mistakes in the distracting atmosphere of a facility performance. Correction would be inappropriate. Try once more, giving the dog enough help to assure success. The people will often applaud enthusiastically for a successful second try. If the second attempt fails, go on to something else.

There's no cause to feel self-conscious when performing with your dog in front of a group. Just keep your mind on your dog. The people couldn't watch you if they tried; all eyes are magnetically drawn to the dog! You'll feel far less nervous as you gain experience.

Whenever possible, I ask the media to show interaction between people and dogs, not tricks. Photographs of the people build their self-esteem and provide other benefits. When media coverage of a therapy dog visit emphasizes tricks, it misses the chance to do something therapeutic for the people in the facility by featuring them. It also creates a misleading impression of therapy dog work.

# 9

# THE HANDLER'S JOB

*Every bit of care you give your dog contributes to therapy dog work. Only the handler can ensure the dog is trained, rested, groomed, socially skilled, and conditioned to the type of handling a particular facility visit is likely to involve.*

The key to successful therapy dog work is the handler. With the right handler, a therapy dog's conditioning and training improve over time on the job. With the right handler, the dog gets the proper care to stay in service as long as possible. The right handler makes the correct decisions about which facilities a dog will serve and when the dog is healthy enough for work.

The public and the facilities need to be able to trust the handler. The lack of good handling can be an insurmountable handicap for even the best of therapy dogs. If people don't trust you, they won't trust your dog, no matter how great the dog.

## ATTITUDE

Years in business taught me a valuable lesson for therapy dog work: attitude. Any job dealing with the public requires a good attitude, and therapy dog handlers need to have remarkable ones. Dog trainers will tell you not to work your dog when you're in a bad mood. This goes double for working a therapy dog around people.

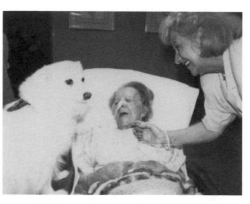

*Working a therapy dog with fragile people requires the handler's total attention and a positive attitude.*

Here are some techniques I use to maintain a good attitude:

1. Control the schedule. I regulate the number of visits on my schedule to stay mentally and emotionally ready, not burned out or tired. If one visit a month is all you have time for, make it faithfully and you will be far more effective than someone who overschedules, breaks commitments, and quits.

2. Get yourself into a good mood on the way to the visit. I sing along with music as I drive. This also warms up my voice and sharpens my timing for working the dog. It's important to get a smile on by the time you walk in the door. Working on your mood is not faking. It will actually improve the way you feel. Acting as if you're happy makes you feel happy. Practice will help your ability to do this. Try to get enough sleep the night before. Have a meal or a snack before the visit, on a schedule to give you stable

blood sugar (the same for your dog). Allow plenty of time to get ready and to make the trip, so you won't arrive late and flustered. If you're late, apologize and then forget it. Don't let it ruin the rest of the visit.

3. Put other things out of your mind and concentrate on your job. It would only take a second for someone to fall because of your dog, or to hurt your dog, or for the dog to accidentally scratch or bruise someone. You can't afford to be inattentive. You simply can't afford to indulge in a bad mood during a visit.

No matter how I feel when I start, I'm in a good mood by the end of the visit. It's a blessing when other things in life aren't going well. I forget my worries and focus on the dog and on the people I'm there to help. The worries are lighter when next I think of them. If there's nothing you can do to control your feelings, you'll need to cancel the visit. It's unsafe to work a dog on a therapy dog visit when you're not in the right mental state. Practice can improve your ability to control moods. If you find you can't control your emotions, therapy dog handling is not the volunteer job for you.

## BE READY TO SAY NO

Sometimes only the handler is in a position to say no. There are at least four things you must be ready to veto. First, be ready to say no to your dog becoming a therapy dog, or continuing to work as one. If you feel your dog wouldn't enjoy therapy dog work, or if you don't feel comfortable handling the dog on visits, your feelings are valid. Don't let anyone talk you into acting against your doubt. If you have a strong desire for this work, explore your feelings until you discover what's causing your doubt. There may be a way to solve it. Lots of people are willing to help you.

You know your dog better than its veterinarian does, or than a dog trainer or instructor could. Sometimes an obedience class instructor may consider a dog okay when the handler doesn't. In obedience class the instructor is in charge and ready to back you, but on therapy dog visits you must be much more self-sufficient as a handler. The obedience instructor may have little or no experience with therapy dog work. Making therapy dog visits and also instructing obedience classes is a lot to ask of anyone! On therapy dog visits, there is much less room for mistakes than in class. Listen to your doubts.

Your veterinarian listens intently to your "feelings" about your dog. What seem like feelings or hunches are often your perceptions of the dog's nonverbal language. The dog has, in its way, told you how it feels. You may not be able to put this knowledge into words, because it doesn't come to you in words. This information is vital, to be respected. If you don't feel your dog is ready to be a therapy dog, say no.

Second, be ready to say no to a particular visit. Your dog may not be feeling well enough to visit, with or without definite symptoms. No dog should be taken on a therapy dog visit when it's ill. This is unfair to the dog and could result in an irritable or sore dog upsetting someone. I saw an example of this change with my dog Star. Years ago, she was ill and in pain for about five weeks. If she even thought I was going to give her a command, she would look at me with desperation, telling me she simply could not obey. She felt cornered at the thought of my giving a command she couldn't perform.

Third, be ready to say no to a particular facility. You may realize a facility doesn't "feel right" for you and your dog. When I had only one small therapy dog, I didn't feel she should work routinely with people who had a lot of mobility without good understanding of their actions, such as preschool children or emotionally disturbed people. After I began working large therapy dogs on such visits, I found this feeling justified. My large dogs were fine for these groups and Angel served them on occasion throughout her career, but physical pressure on the small dogs was too great for me to have wanted to work her there routinely.

And last, be ready to say no to something someone wants to do to your dog. If you feel your dog shouldn't be worked by people other than you, say no. If you feel a particular person might mistreat your dog, keep your dog away from the person. Don't let anyone "test" your therapy dog in a way you disapprove. If a staff member or other person suggests or even orders you to work your dog in a way you feel is unsafe or unfair to your dog, say no. If something goes wrong and someone gets hurt, you are held accountable and could even lose your dog. If someone traumatizes your dog, you'll be the one with the job of rehabilitating the dog. These facts put you in charge of how your dog is handled.

This doesn't mean to refuse to keep your dog on leash if asked, which will neither harm the dog, nor deprive you of exerting control and supervision. Saying no means you have the right and the responsibility to protect your dog. It has to be you, because no one else can. When your dog is tired, thirsty, being upset by someone, uncomfortable or at risk, it's your job to take care of the dog.

## WATER

Every therapy dog handler needs to understand a dog's need for water. The dog's only natural means of cooling itself is by giving off moisture through the mouth and nose. Dogs don't perspire like humans, except a little through the footpads. A dog in perfect condition shouldn't work in temperatures above 85 degrees. If the dog has any physical problem, is not an athlete, has a heavy coat, has a shortened muzzle or is getting along in years, the top working temperature should be lower.

*Water sprayed into the mouth and on the coat can protect a dog from dangerous effects of overheating, and reduce stress.*

Nursing homes are quite warm, because inactive people easily feel cold and are susceptible to hypothermia. Especially in summer, it may be too hot in a nursing home to ask your dog to entertain. It may also be too hot to get the dog there safely, unless you have air-conditioned transportation. As your dog's age and physical condition changes, its heat tolerance changes, too, and you'll need to adjust visits accordingly.

Adequate water to keep the body cooling system working properly is vital to a therapy dog's safety. Any spill in a facility can cause someone to slip and fall, so be fussy about mopping up drips. Also mop any spots on a smooth floor where your dog drools. I carry one towel for this purpose, and a second towel to place on a lap or furniture before my dog sits or lies there. You may also need a towel to wipe people's hands after your dog licks them. Launder towels after each visit. I carry towels and other items in a shoulder bag.

Using a spray bottle, you can spritz a dog with water, especially on the head, tummy and chest. If you're in the sun, spritz the dog's back, too. I think of this as "artificial sweat." It allows the dog to benefit from the same evaporative cooling human perspiration provides. This technique can make your dog more comfortable. The method won't work in high humidity, or make it reasonable to work any dog in unsafe conditions.

Carry the water in whatever manner works best for you and your dog. Some dogs want to drink from a dish, while others may refuse, even when you know they need water. In such cases, I spray water into the dog's mouth. The need for water on therapy dog visits is one reason I prefer never to use a spray bottle as a correction device with a dog.

Some handlers use sports bottles to give their dogs water. I've also had good results with plastic squeeze bottles. Gabriel loves to eat the small ice cubes readily available at all the facilities he and I currently visit. Ice provides a powerful cooling effect!

## WHAT TO WEAR

Since working a dog is a physical task, dress comfortably, but nothing revealing, scruffy or soiled. Therapy dog handlers need not dress as formally as administrative personnel in a facility, but can dress more like those who provide the physical care to the people.

I wear an identification tag on therapy dog visits, and therapy dog identification on the dog. It makes sense for everyone in a facility to wear identification for security reasons. Office supply stores sell plastic holders to clip onto clothing. You can slip your ID card inside. I suggest the card say "Volunteer Therapy Dog Handler" and your name. People you encounter in the facility need to know you are there as a volunteer.

Since I have visited psychiatric facilities where last names are kept private for confidentiality reasons, I have my last name on the bottom of the tag. I have a piece of cardstock cut to fit over the last name so I can slip that into place for a visit to a facility where I need it.

For the dog, some therapy dog groups specify the identification each dog is to wear. The facility will appreciate ID on the therapy dog, because it helps them explain the dog's presence. To protect confidentiality on psychiatric visits, I cover the dog's ID tags with masking tape. I learned the necessity of this precaution when a psychiatric patient read my phone number from the dog's tag and called my home. Staff and volunteers in psychiatric facilities are cautioned to keep phone numbers and other such information confidential.

What about costumes on therapy dogs? Some people claim costumes embarrass dogs. I doubt it. When a dog seems to dislike a costume, it's probably uncomfortable or the dog hasn't been properly introduced to it. I felt it necessary for Saint to wear a colorful, ruffled clown collar on all therapy dog visits. It made an enormous difference in his appearance, and kept most people from being uncomfortable around him. It saved a lot of time I would otherwise have used to put people at ease, and it relieved people's fears. The collar was part of his uniform for visits.

A flowing or ruffled collar around the neck is a simple way to soften the dog's appearance without interfering with movement or comfort. A bandanna around the dog's neck does little to make the dog look less intimidating. Choose any costume carefully to avoid overheating the dog.

My therapy dogs have all worn a harness on visits, with a therapy dog patch stitched at the top. I much prefer this to a coat or cape, since therapy dogs are there for petting, and the harness leaves maximum fur available to be touched. A coat, cape or t-shirt can also be inhumane if it overheats the therapy dog. What is comfortable for one dog may be unkind to another, since breeds vary widely in heat tolerance.

*Some health-care programs are only open during the day, and therefore need handlers who can bring therapy dogs then.*

## TIMES OF DAY

Another part of the handler's job is to decide what time of day to go on therapy dog visits, and how long visits should last. While beginners shouldn't work longer than an hour, experienced dogs and handlers may make longer visits, especially in facilities they visit frequently where the dog feels at ease. You may not have a choice about the time of day, if a group leader does the scheduling, if the facility's schedule is restrictive or if your work schedule allows only one particular time for visits. If your own schedule is limited, you may find some facilities can't accommodate it, but others will. People will probably respond to your dog no matter when you come, if you come consistently and do a good job.

For nursing homes, I've found weekday mornings ideal. On weekdays, the staff is usually in full force. In the morning, people are less sleepy and cranky than in the afternoon. Staff members in nursing homes tell me people are noticeably more responsive to the dogs in the mornings. Additionally, if we can reach people early, improved moods last the rest of the day, even longer for some.

I also find my dogs tend to play in the morning and sleep in the afternoon at home. Dogs sleep about fourteen hours a day. When we go on visits in the mornings and the dogs take their regular afternoon naps, I don't find them tired out by visits. Morning visits also provide the opportunity to use the facility's lunchtime to end your visit. Otherwise it can be hard to leave.

Weekend, evening and afternoon programs can all be successful. One advantage is more involvement with family members. A disadvantage is when staff has to come in on their time off for weekend and evening visits. Sometimes they fail to appear, a major problem when your program requires staff help.

Some facilities, such as schools, are only in session on weekdays. Therapists in rehabilitation settings tend to work in the daytime, so therapy dogs working with them need daytime schedules, too. As therapy dog work gains recognition in communities, perhaps some employers will arrange work schedules so their employees who are volunteer therapy dog handlers can make these daytime visits.

## LIMITS

How much a dog is allowed to work should be carefully limited, and this, too, is the handler's job. It falls on you because no one else can know the dog well enough or control its other activities to make the needed decisions. The settings where the dog works, the dog's other activities and the type of dog will all be factors.

Some therapy dog visits are quite stressful for the dog. People in facilities who aren't aware of the consequences of their actions and yet move around a lot will represent a great challenge to both handler and dog. If the people sometimes become violent, the situation can become dangerous and the dog will be aware of its jeopardy. Sometimes you can predict the difficult visits, and sometimes they come unexpectedly. Select carefully where you are and are not willing to work with your particular dog.

The dog will also experience less stress on one- or two-dog visits than on visits with several other dogs. The more other dogs there, and the more dogs strange to your dog, the more stress. Groups need limits for the number of dogs on a visit. Six to twelve dogs are plenty for most situations.

Whenever you feel a visit may have pushed your dog too hard, give the dog at least a two-week break from therapy dog visits, and during the break give the dog happy outings. Do this before the dog shows any sign of burnout.

Build your schedule gradually. You might choose to make one or two visits a month for the first six months to a year. This provides time to enhance your beginner dog's training between visits. Throughout my dogs' careers, I have found a limit of no more than an average of one visit per week for each dog has worked well. When Star grew older, I reduced the frequency of her visits. Saint remained comfortable at the same frequency of visits, but toward the end I worked him in situations less stressful on an old dog's joints.

Enthusiasm makes volunteers eager to start full-force. In some pursuits, it's only ourselves we risk overworking. In therapy dog work, the handler's job as keeper of the dog makes it essential to resist the gung-ho attitude of pushing forward at any cost. Overworked therapy dogs may develop diarrhea, start avoiding touch by people, and ultimately will have no choice but to growl in an effort to stop the pressure they can no longer endure. A slow start lets the dog get used to the situation and develop a real love for it. Therapy dog work benefits most from handlers and dogs who can stay in it for the long term, which is most likely with dogs whose handlers diligently protect them from overwork.

## ATTENTION ON DOG, POTENTIAL INJURIES

It's the handler's job to pay total attention to the dog on a therapy dog visit. If you have not yet trained a dog, you will find this skill requires practice. The first night of any beginning obedience class is scary, because the handlers haven't yet learned to pay attention to their dogs. Eventually trainers learn, with practice, but you always have to discipline your mind to it.

This handling skill is like driving a car. You can't watch every part of the road at all times, but

*Spreading a towel on a person's lap under the dog helps prevent any scratches from the dog's toenails.*

you develop habits such as checking both ways before turning left or crossing an intersection, scanning the road ahead both near and far, keeping your eyes on the stoplight while stopped waiting for it to change, checking your speed at intervals, and

*With a child right under her face and gripping her front legs, Star might have felt stressed, especially since there was another child touching from her left. Her face tells the story. Star was at ease with children.*

poising your foot over the brake when passing a child. A therapy dog handler's habits are similar. Just as inattention when driving can cause an accident, inattention when handling a dog around people might result in a mistake.

It's a twofold responsibility—controlling the dog and protecting the dog. When working with certain people, protecting the dog will take priority. When working a small dog, this responsibility takes most of the handler's attention. A major means of protecting your dog is to use training to control the dog, to see trouble coming and to dodge it. Controlling the dog and protecting the dog go together.

If your dog is easygoing or highly trained, it may be tempting for you to let the dog work on its own with little of your attention. This would be a mistake. The dog doesn't understand the hazards, nor do the people. Only a skilled handler can manage the dog to keep everyone safe. With an easy-to-handle dog, the handler may not appear to work hard physically. But the handler must always be mentally at work, ready to use perhaps just a quiet word to guide the dog to safety.

The best way to explain how the handler needs to exert control is to give examples of what could go wrong, and how a handler can avoid or deal with each situation. The most likely serious accident resulting from a dog in a facility is a fall. Falls are common accidents even without dogs. Falls involving dogs usually happen when a dog is in a facility with no handler, commonly a resident dog rather than a volunteer visiting with a therapy dog.

Don't expect a dog to figure out how to stay out of the way. Staff members run all sorts of errands in the facility, sometimes pushing heavy equipment. They may be able to see around equipment well enough to avoid a standing person or a person seated in a wheelchair, but not a dog on the floor. If you have a dog in your house, you may realize how hard it can be to avoid tripping over it. Some dogs dodge better than others; little dogs try harder, and herding dogs notice movement more. It's the handler's job to watch traffic.

I don't like my dog standing too near unsteady people walking, standing up from a seated position, or in the process of taking a seat. If there is no time to move the dog, steady Stays become precious.

Other opportunities for people to fall with therapy dogs come when a frail person takes the leash to walk the dog. The person could fall over the dog, tangle in the leash, step on the dog or otherwise have a mishap. If you don't feel comfortable letting others walk your dog, say no.

You can intervene when another person unexpectedly takes your dog's leash by grasping the leash yourself between the person's hand and the dog's collar. If the person pulls too hard, your hand can buffer pressure on the dog, and you can buffer pressure on the person if the dog pulls. On a few occasions, I have had people pull the leash so hard that the best recourse for me was to disconnect the leash from the dog's collar. This is one of the times you need reliable off-leash control.

Your dog's body language, especially the face, can tell you if anything is upsetting the dog. A relaxed expression with the mouth open and light panting is good. I think of it as a relaxation response. If that isn't the dog's expression, make sure you know exactly what the people around your dog are doing. Check all sides. The dog may just be alerting to something, or it may be extremely cool, but check.

Heel and Swing Finish commands will help you keep the dog out of people's way and will reduce the risk of falls. This kind of control will distinguish you as a safe handler and will be much preferred by the staff. Since people will congregate around the dog, stay alert to keep hallways and other passages clear.

Another potential accident is a dog scratching a person with its toenails. For certain people, a scratch can be slow to heal or can get infected. There could also be confusion about whether the scratch came from toenail or tooth. To guard against this injury, groom your dog's toenails, removing sharp edges as well as excess length. I trim my dogs' toenails every week to keep them short and smooth.

Make sure there is sufficient padding to prevent injury between your small dog's feet and a person's skin if you put a dog on someone's lap. Use your extra towel if necessary. Don't have your large dog put any weight on people, even if they ask you to do it.

If your dog shakes hands or otherwise paws at people, monitor this behavior, and when necessary, guide the dog's foot when near a person's skin. Make sure your dog doesn't step or lean on people's feet. Don't set even a small dog on a person who is extremely thin or frail.

Another potential injury may occur when there is accidental contact between the dog's teeth and someone's hands. Besides retrieving games, this can happen when people give the dog food, as discussed in Chapter Eight. If you wish to let people feed your therapy dog on visits, be sure your dog gets the appropriate training. If, like me, you prefer people not to feed your therapy dog, tell them at every opportunity. They won't see it as a personal rejection if you are consistent and give them the reasons. I tell them Gabriel gets a small meal before and after the visit, and is calmer on the job when not expecting people to feed him.

Children in a dog's face represent a special case for handler caution. Keep a hand on the dog, and don't let a face-to-face encounter last too long. Focus your attention on the dog, with someone else supervising the children. If a situation becomes very intense, you may want to gently hold the dog's face right into your face, cradling it with your hands and speaking softly to the dog.

When more than one dog visits at the same time, handlers must obviously prevent the dogs from fighting. But even play between dogs can cause injury to people, as dogs tussle with each other and fail to see people in the way.

Another potential accident is when a disoriented person grabs the dog and won't let go. The person may grab feet, ears, tail or the whole dog. Of course, if you see this might happen, the best thing to do is to keep the dog out of the person's reach. No one is helped by being allowed to abuse a dog. Besides hurting the dog and possibly ruining it as a therapy dog, the person may lose friends in the facility as a result of such an incident.

When the worst happens and you find your dog being clutched by someone, your first concern is to keep the dog calm. Get the dog focused on your voice. Hold the dog steady. You may want to encircle the dog's muzzle with one hand. Scratch the dog behind the ears as you would during an injection, to distract its pain senses. Massaging a muscle deeply with your hand may help. Avoid shouting or making any sudden movement which could trigger your dog to try and protect itself or you. If you must call for help, keep panic out of your voice. Lift your chin and project your voice so it will carry, but don't let it convey fear to your dog.

If you can get staff help, let the staff member pry the person's hands away, while you give your full support to the dog. If you can't get help, hold the dog's focus with your voice while you steadily pry the clutching hands away.

With experience, you will be able to avoid almost all such incidents, which is why a therapy dog working with an experienced handler faces far less stress than with a beginning handler.

In the unlikely event of a therapy dog biting someone, follow the requirements of the facility and the therapy dog group. Rendering aid immediately and showing sincere concern reduces the risk of a lawsuit later. Always carry identification and proof of a veterinarian-administered rabies vaccination when you work a dog in public. You may have to surrender your dog for quarantine at a shelter or veterinary hospital, at your expense.

After a dog bite, the handler, any group he or she represents and the facility could be liable to lawsuit. This is one reason you need to keep your therapy dog registration in good standing with a therapy dog registry that provides liability insurance. Several factors would make you more likely to be sued or to lose a lawsuit. If the dog has had any training to bite humans, has known aggressive tendencies, was out of control at the time or lacks training, your liability could be increased. Owners of large dogs, especially breeds perceived as aggressive, are more vulnerable to lawsuit, as are handlers who are being paid.

Obviously you don't want your therapy dog to bite anyone. The best protection against such a terrible experience is your constant attention to the dog on therapy dog visits. The most likely cause of a dog bite would be if someone hurt or terrified the dog and it felt cornered and unprotected. Be there for your dog.

Handler attention is also a major consideration in whether or not you should take more than one dog on a therapy dog visit. It's physically impossible to give your full attention to more than one dog working at once. You will achieve more by taking one dog on a visit and giving it your full attention than you would with extra dogs and no other handlers to support them.

If you train your dogs to be handled by others, a staff person might handle an extra dog you bring on a therapy dog visit. That would leave it to you to supervise. You might also bring an extra volunteer who doesn't have a therapy dog or whose dog is out of service for some reason to handle one of your dogs.

There are cases where dogs work closely as a team for one handler. This would be a matter of special training and extreme caution. It is more common in performance-type visits. Therapy dog registries usually require that each therapy dog to be accompanied by a handler who has passed the organization's testing with that dog.

## ZOONOTIC DISEASES

You'll often see news stories touting diseases, called "zoonotic diseases," that people can catch from dogs. It's in keeping with our alarmist news media to capture people's attention with scary headlines, in the quest to attract wider audiences and advertising dollars.

The truth is that few problems are transmitted from dogs to humans. Most such situations result from dogs who have been in situations of poor care. These include newly adopted dogs where the new owners don't fully know the health status. Immunocompromised people should not be exposed to a dog from an animal shelter or pet store until a quarantine period of at least two weeks has passed, plus whatever additional time is needed to resolve health problems that emerge.

When properly managed therapy dogs are taken on visits to health-care facilities, the incidence of disease transmission is virtually zero.

What does proper management mean?

1. Don't take a dog with fleas or ticks on a therapy dog visit.

2. Keep your dog currently registered with a national therapy dog registry, which will require you to have health checks and vaccinations performed on schedule.

3. Keep your dog home from therapy dog visits if the dog is in any way unwell. When in doubt, keep it out! If the dog has any diarrhea, even in the absence of other symptoms, that dog must not visit until the situation is diagnosed and resolved. The same goes for any broken skin, since a few skin problems can be transmitted from dogs to people.

4. Whenever your dog visits the veterinarian for any illness, injury or surgery, specifically ask the veterinarian if this problem means you should keep the dog out of therapy dog visits. If the veterinarian says it's not a problem, but you still don't feel confident about it, don't take the dog! As a therapy dog handler, you are also managing the dog's stress, and your doubts may be due to the fact that you have a better understanding of your dog and of the visitation situation than your veterinarian has.

5. You pose a greater risk of spreading disease on a therapy dog visit than your dog does! Never go into a health-care facility when you have a respiratory or other contagious virus. If you are working with especially immunocompromised people, cooperate with the facility to arrange any extra testing they feel is necessary on you and/or your dog.

*Always get permission before putting a dog on anyone's bed. In this case, it was the only way the lady could reach Star. I spread a clean towel on the bed before putting Star there.*

## TERRITORIAL RANGES – SPACE FOR EVERYONE

Another aspect of the handler's job is understanding territorial ranges and using them to advantage. People have territorial ranges for various situations, and so do dogs.

### Fearful People

Working your dog in public on social skills will prepare you to "read" people's faces and decide whether or not they feel at ease with your dog. You can learn through experience and by watching people's faces and body language how far you need to stay back with the dog to avoid making them uncomfortable. Six feet is enough for some, twenty feet or more for others. Listen to comments to help determine space, too. If someone says they are allergic or afraid, or tells you another person present has one of these problems, this information takes priority over any body language you might observe.

At the right distance, the person can see your body language and the dog's, but won't feel threatened. Try positions-in-place. Perhaps later the person will feel like petting the dog, but no one should be pressured.

You can also move outside the territorial range to interact with other people with the dog, and see if this puts the fearful person at ease. Some people aren't actually afraid, just somewhat "goosey." It can be part of a medical problem, or even behavior the person has developed to get attention. With experience you'll learn to recognize this.

Regardless of their reasons, people should never have a dog forced on them. Consider the territorial range their space, not yours.

If you encounter someone who persists in jokes that represent the dog as aggressive, politely ask them not to say such things. Representing a therapy dog as a danger is not funny and can jeopardize your work. When a person tries to provoke an aggressive reaction from your dog with idiotic behavior, use the attention exercise to help your dog ingnore it.

### Give The Dog Room To Move Away

Saint taught me something about the dog's territorial range. One day we visited a preschool for children with disabilities. A tiny boy crawled around fast, drooling profusely. At first, he and Saint mutually enjoyed having Saint wash his face. But when the child crawled at Saint and backed the dog up about twenty feet, Saint decided to stop him.

Saint didn't bite, snap or growl. But he said something to the child in a fraction of a second. The child burst into tears. The teacher told the child how far faces need to be apart. (I gathered the child had this problem with people.) I took Saint's muzzle instantly and spoke to him quietly, my nose to his, to remind him it wasn't his job to correct children. Whatever it was he did, he never did it again.

This is an example of how the handler must protect the dog so the dog won't decide to take responsibility for the situation. Saint treated the child as he would have treated a puppy. He was extremely gentle with puppies, small dogs and children. He would not have hurt the child, except by accident. Since he was accustomed to having people in his face, an accidental injury would have been unlikely. Being well-prepared allowed us to survive my handler error. If the same situation happened now with Gabriel, who weighs about twelve pounds less than Saint weighed, and has the typical agility of a Belgian Tervuren, I could command him "Up, on Me" and lift him in my arms above the child. He jumps as I lift, making this a maneuver we can execute quickly. If it happened with Believer, I'd simply have her do "Paws Up" to my arm. She's a tall girl!

This experience and others taught me not to allow anyone to corner the dog. The therapy dog needs room to move away if someone puts too much pressure on it. The handler can't always be sure exactly how much pressure the dog is feeling.

**Protecting The Dog's Territorial Range Means Watching Out For The Following:**
1. If you need to physically position the dog, get the dog set and then remove your physical pressure. Move back if the dog wants to move away from a person.
2. Don't let a crowd surround your dog. When working a therapy dog in a large group of people, stay on your feet and circulate, dealing with a few people at a time.
3. Don't get backed up against a wall, where you and the dog have no escape from a press of people.
4. Your dog may enjoy having several people pet it at once, but be especially alert at such times. It's easy to overlook the one hand inflicting pain on the dog. Avoid having too many small children petting the dog at one time. Three or four is about the limit with children under school age. They aren't always gentle, and their faces are right in the dog's face.
5. Don't let people keep coming at the dog. Get staff help with the people if necessary.

Other helpful aspects regarding "territory" are methods to use space and to position your dog to more effectively help people. As the following techniques reveal, space is an integral part of the body language dogs and people use to communicate.

*Saint and Emma loved relaxing together when he visited her.*

## Put Yourself On The Other Person's Level

Put yourself on the same level as the person you are talking to, whenever possible. Seated people then don't have to bend their necks to look up at you, and they feel your willingness to take unhurried time with them. Remain ready to pop up at any moment that good dog handling might require you to stand.

## Use The Dog's Placement To Reach People

Putting the dog in a different location can increase a person's response. Some people respond strongly to a dog on their laps, when it's safe. If not, you can sit next to people and hold the dog on your lap so they can reach it. This has a completely different effect than a dog on the floor. I've also seen great responses from people when I place a dog on furniture near them. I typically use a chair or sofa.

I put a towel on the furniture under the dog. The towel catches hair, and eliminates complaints about the dog being on furniture. On vinyl surfaces, a towel would slip, creating an unsafe situation for the dog. In this case, it may be best to put the dog directly on the chair or sofa, and carefully brush away any hair afterward with your hand. I lift or help the dog down, to minimize joint stress. Be sure, too, to put walkers, bed trays, chairs and any other items back where you found them, if you have to move anything to get your dog into position for someone to reach it.

Another way to position the dog is to have it lie on its back. Angel loved to loll on her back in my arms. This ap-

*Just seeing Angel held this way brought smiles to many faces.*

peals to people—and well it might, because a dog in this position demonstrates submissiveness and total trust. It puts people at ease with the dog. Dogs too large to hold this way may lie on their backs on the floor for petting, a position Saint took occasionally on visits. This also touches a chord in people. Protect your dog when lying on its back, because mistreatment in such an ultrasubmissive position on the floor could destroy the dog's trust. Don't force a dog to lie on its back on a therapy dog visit—it must be the dog's choice.

### Work The Dog to Attract and Direct People's Attention

Your dog's presence in the facility has a profound effect in some other ways, too:

1. When a dog walks in, all eyes will turn to it. If another program is in progress, keep the dog around the corner or otherwise out of sight until the program is finished. The dog walking in would seriously disrupt the other program.

2. When people need to move toward the dining room or elsewhere for specific care, you can help the staff by leading the way with the dog (up to the acceptable boundary—not into the dining room when food is being served) to get people to follow.

3. During some procedures, such as psychological testing for children, the dog's presence could be a severe distraction. One way to handle this is to have the dog in a quiet Down-Stay behind some sort of screen. I've used an upended mini-trampoline to good effect, or a large filing cabinet. It helps if the handler can see both the dog and the activity in the area. Use an area through which no one will need to pass.

4. It may not be a good idea to have your dog bark on commmand in a facility. Many people find a dog's bark frightening, even if they asked you to have the dog bark. Some people in the room may have limited vision or understanding.

I remember one visit when I asked Angel to bark on command and noticed people were less interested in petting her for the rest of the visit. I've seen little children burst into tears and elderly people get terrified looks on their faces at the bark of a large dog. You can't always be sure they fully understand your

*Angel loved working from her platform. She was out from under people's feet, easy for everyone to reach but not squeeze, and cooler than when held for petting.*

explanation of the barking. Some dogs consider barking, even on command, somewhat aggressive. When you encourage the dog to bark around people, you may encourage it to take the wrong attitude toward those people.

Barking also makes noise that may be unwelcome in a facility. Use barking cautiously, if at all. Move the dog well back from people before cuing it to bark. Therapy dogs are generally most effective when they do not show behaviors such as barking on the job.

### Help for Small Dogs

One technique I found invaluable when working small Angel was to set her up on a platform. You can design your own, depending on your dog and the materials available to you. I used a high-quality vinyl pet carrier. I strapped it to a dolly made to fit, with swivel wheels, using an elastic luggage strap. I attached towels to the back of the crate with another strap, and carried Angel's other gear inside. The crate's knobby surface gave her good footing. It put her at a comfortable height for people in wheelchairs or standing erect to pet her. Angel did a flawless Wait on this platform; if your dog will not, you need to work differently.

The popular image of small therapy dogs is sitting on laps. In reality, most people can't hold a dog on their laps. Some are too frail, some sit with laps steeply inclined so the dog can't balance there, and some clutch roughly at the dog when it's seated on them. With Angel on her platform, she was easy to reach, the person didn't bear her weight and she was spared the risk of being held or dropped. When it was appropriate for her to sit on a lap, I offered to spread a towel there first (if

*Paws Up is not only helpful in getting the dog positioned for petting, but is also a reward for the dog, when combined with a hug from you.*

the person's clothing was thin, I insisted on the towel for padding), and I lifted her. Sometimes she could step across from the platform to the lap, on my cue.

She stopped getting tired on visits when I started using the platform. This was partly because she no longer had to dodge people's feet. On her platform, no one could trip over her, a safety benefit for people, too. The risk of anyone squeezing the little dog was reduced, since she was close to one of their hands but not to the other. Angel interacted with people more expressively from the platform than she could when held for petting. It's an effective way for a small dog to work.

I let Angel jump up onto the platform, but I lifted her down. This spared her joints the impact of the jump, and encouraged her to think of getting down as under my control, not hers.

## Teach A Paws Up Command

Due to his height, I have used Paws Up more with Gabriel than with my previous dogs. With his back to me, I can hold a front paw in each hand, and support his hips with my knees. This is an extremely stable, controlled position, with physical as well as emotional support to the dog. Believer is taller than Gabriel, and I'm pleased that she is going to be even easier for some of the people to reach.

It's best to make it your strict policy to never allow your large dog's paws on a person. Watch out for walkers, too, since they can tip over with the dog's weight.

## Older Dogs May Require Special Positioning

Sometimes arthritis means retirement for a therapy dog, but it depends on the dog and the type of visit. Saint visited nursing homes to age thirteen and a half, with careful handling from me. He showed no pain from walking or being petted anywhere on his body, but we discontinued the visits to groups of small children to protect him from the occasional child whose parents have thoughtlessly taught him or her to ride a dog like a horse. Star took over those visits.

Walking on slick floors becomes more difficult for older dogs, and sitting on such floors may no longer be possible for them. They slip backwards and have to "pedal" with the front feet to remain in a sitting position. It may seem funny, but it would not be humane to require the dog to hold the position. I did find I could stand behind Saint with my feet in a "Charlie Chaplin" position and support him in a Sit. But most of the time it made more sense to let him stand or lie down instead, whichever he chose.

We reduced Paws Up situations to brief greetings, and eliminated Paws Up entirely for about the last year of his work. This prevented some direct contact with people in high beds where Saint would have had to stand on hind legs for the person to reach him. If I stood in a quiet room talking about dogs with a resident while Saint lay on the cool floor resting until we moved on to the next room, people seemed to still enjoy his coming. Most of the people in the nursing homes could reach him from wheelchairs, chairs, and low beds without rails.

### Orienting the Dog to the Area

If your therapy dog is a beginner, you may find it gets overexcited and silly when you first arrive at a facility. The cure for this is a brief session of warm-up exercises.

Saint needed this for a few months. In time, the dog shifts into working gear without it. The routine I used started with Heel, tuning him to working at my side. Then I had Saint Come, tuning him to working with me at a distance. A sidewalk, parking lot or quiet hallway will all do nicely for this short review. It should be upbeat, fast to focus the dog's attention, and just long enough to get the dog into gear without tiring.

If the dog likes to walk ahead, like Gabriel, I emphasize loose leash from the time we get out of the car. I used left turns a lot with Saint, because those required him to move out of my way.

Saint was a genuinely hyperactive dog who entered therapy dog work later in life when training had given him and me the necessary finesse. He needed a longer warm-up, but only for about six months.

Gabriel is a steady fellow who only needs me to consistently follow through on commands, and give an extra one now and then to aid his understanding and reorient his attention. Angel and Star didn't need a warm-up. Believer at this point is so young that she needs a warm-up and extra help from me throughout the visit, shaping her habits for the future.

Another common problem is the dog breaking off its work to go sniff corners. This is easy to solve if you look at it from the dog's point of view. Give the dog a quick tour when you first enter the room. It actually saves time, and the dog will work work much better for you. You'll learn to carry this out efficiently, and people will easily understand your explanation. Tell them the dog needs to get its bearings. Humans have the same need, but we can satisfy it by looking around a room, while most dogs use their noses more than their eyes.

I noticed Saint had an extra need to sniff people when seasons would change. This happened mainly with people in day programs who went home at night. Human bodies change rather profoundly to adapt to changing seasons. Don't let your dog give someone a physical examination with its nose! But don't be surprised if your dog seems especially sniffy some days. Keep the dog's behavior within bounds, and explain it to the people. Most of them will be fascinated.

Star liked to orient with her eyes, and the fastest method was to lift her in my arms for a brief look around the room. This helped her on one occasion in particular, in a room with television lights and cameras.

## HANDLER AS INTERPRETER

One of the hats we wear as therapy dog handlers is "interpreter." I interpret the dog's behavior for people. I also interpret the situation for the dog, to direct it into the proper behavior. It amazes me what interpretations people will make based on a dog's actions. I've had people think the dog wanted to bite them because it licked, sniffed or looked at them. After I explain what the dog's behavior means, these people are often instantly at ease.

Some behaviors need to be handled rather than interpreted. If your dog starts to bathe its posterior with its tongue, get it to stop. Distracting the dog usually works. Scratching doesn't look good, either, and it's not good for your dog's skin. Mounting another dog or a person is unacceptable on a therapy dog visit, and indicates a need for more training.

If your dog will need to relieve itself on a visit, take it to an appropriate place before entering and for any necessary breaks. The time to develop your dog's control and understanding is during outings when you practice social skills. Be ready to clean up after your dog in a facility in case of an accident, but with a properly trained dog you may never have to clean up except outdoors. None of my dogs have ever had an accident in a facility, but I still carry plastic bags in my pocket. I did recently have the experience of Believer throwing up on a visit. I caught it in her water dish and flushed it down a toilet.

*Star enjoyed being petted while she satisfied her herding dog curiosity by gazing around the room. As her interpreter, I was able to truthfully assure people that she loved the petting.*

Licking people can give therapeutic benefits, and some people enjoy it. As interpreter, you can tell people licking is a sign of affection. Don't let the dog lick people right on the mouth, as there can be a slight risk of transmitting disease. At the first sign of someone not wanting to be licked, redirect the dog's attention.

Sniffing calls for varied handling. Of course the dog shouldn't be allowed to sniff people's crotches. Since sniffing is natural dog behavior used in social interaction, sometimes it's appropriate to allow the dog to sniff politely as part of a greeting. As interpreter, explain why dogs do this: dogs get more information by sniffing than people get with their eyes. This information helps dogs relate effectively to people. If people are comfortable with the sniffing, it can even make them feel singled out for special attention.

Saint, a retired tracking dog, sniffed people's knees, then offered his head for petting. He didn't seem to have an opinion about the scent, just a need to check it. In most situations, it was better to interpret for him than to alter a natural behavior people so easily accepted. Note, though, it's part of a greeting. If the person isn't being greeted by the dog, they won't get sniffed, either. The dog should not be allowed to touch or get near anyone unless the person wishes.

Interpreting for a dog is more natural than you may realize. People often "talk for" dogs. Two people will speak back and forth, for the dog. This isn't silly. It's an attempt to verbalize a dog's nonverbal language. When at the veterinarian's office, on a therapy dog visit or elsewhere with a dog, I find this happens a lot. Other people often initiate it, including the veterinarian. It helps humans to better understand a dog's behavior, feelings and point of view.

## WHAT TO SAY ON YOUR VISITS

Sometimes people are at a loss for words when facing a stranger who may not be able to speak fluently. It helps to have options in your mind in advance.

Of course the first thing is to ask (or to assess through body language) "Do you like dogs?" This helps you determine whether the person wants your dog near or not. You might still carry on a conversation with someone while keeping your dog six to ten feet away from them, but where to place the dog is usually the first thing to determine. I once had someone ask me how to get her dog used to dead bodies. When I asked her to explain, it turned out she had twice walked into rooms with her dog where the person in the bed was deceased. If you look for some sign in the person's voice, face or body language BEFORE you walk in with your dog, obviously this will not happen!

Once the person is petting the dog, the conversation is likely to steer toward this dog, and possibly toward other dogs the person has had. I like to point out whenever a person is especially pleasing the dog with petting. I also interpret for the dog, if the dog is looking at something, turns a certain way, etc.

Sometimes people will inquire about the dog's lifestyle, because they love dogs, and they wonder if they should be worrying about this dog. I find that saying "Gabriel sleeps on my bed" answers most concerns. He's not going to be stolen or lost, be-

*It's unspeakably painful when a beloved dog dies. The joy of working with Gabriel was the perfect medicine for my wounded heart. You and your therapy dog will comfort many people who have experienced the loss of a dog.*

cause when he's outside, he's in a fenced yard and I am watching him. He eats four times a day, and he is fully combed out every day. Knowing that, people relax and enjoy the visit, free from worry about the dog.

You will encounter people who mourn the fact that they can't have a dog anymore. It helps them if you talk about the work involved with a dog. Those who have had dogs in the past will immediately remember the work, and the conversation will help them switch from the emotional aspects of dog ownership to the practical ones. Most of my therapy dogs have been furry, which underscores my point about the work of grooming. I can also tell so many stories about dog mischief! Dog mischief is a great topic of conversation in general, and my dogs keep me well supplied with stories!

Let's say the person is not petting your dog, but seems to enjoy your company. What do you talk about? Remember that you are not there in the capacity of doctor or psychotherapist. It would not be appropriate to give people specific medical advice, or to psychoanalyze them. It is helpful to encourage people that they can feel better if they participate in the therapy available to them at the facility. It is also helpful to join them in positive conversation about anything they wish to discuss.

People with Alzheimer's disease can become upset when they get confused. Be clear, keep concepts simple, and keep an upbeat attitude. Do not get into any arguments, but do try to help them stay oriented to reality. Be careful not to startle anyone with your touch. If you are going to touch people, let them see your touch coming.

If someone cannot see, gently give whatever direction is needed to pet the dog. If someone cannot hear well, project your voice by lifting your chin as you speak. Let the person see your mouth when you talk, and of course be prepared to repeat yourself. Whenever it's possible for staff or family members to help in such situations, the result can be more comfortable communication. You will find that gaining experience makes it easier for you to communicate with people.

When visiting psychiatric units, do not give out your last name or specific personal information that would allow a person to locate you outside the facility. You will not be told anyone's diagnosis or history, and you might be conversing with someone who is there to be evaluated on a criminal charge. Do not discuss religion in any depth in psychiatric settings, because, sadly, some people have psychological problems in this area.

You will probably be instructed to visit with people in supervised areas rather than go with them to their rooms, and this is important advice. You may also be asked to sign a confidentiality agreement. Whether or not this is asked of you, be faithful about the privacy of the people you meet in psychiatric care settings. Their livelihoods or relationships could be harmed by others knowing they have received such care. You have an obligation not to divulge the identities of the people to anyone outside that setting.

Therapy dog visits are not the place to sell other services you might have to offer, such as training, grooming, or puppies for sale, so be aware of that in your conversations.

Sometimes people will speak in detail about getting a dog when they get out of the facility. You often will not know the prognosis, so be careful about overly encouraging such plans.

You will hear disturbing stories about how people have treated dogs. Remember that, even if you have a serious commitment to animal welfare and to responsible dog management, there is only so much you can appropriately say about it in this setting. Keep it positive.

Your goal is to facilitate people's enjoyment of your dog's visit, and of your being there, too. You may see other things in the environment to spark conversation, such as artwork the folks have created, loving touches in their rooms from family members, and activities in the facility. Whatever else there is to talk about, the dog will give you a natural conversation starter with most people.

Sometimes people will complain to you about the food or other aspects of life in the facility. My personal view is that I need to let staff know if I encounter an immediate need—such as a person who has fallen, or requires help to the bathroom, etc.

Inspecting a health-care facility is a trained role that I am not there to perform. So I let people blow off a little steam if they want to talk about something, and then I either excuse myself or steer the conversation into a more positive vein. I have never found it necessary to report anything to legal authorities, but of course you should do so if you ever have good reason to believe abuse is occurring.

People will often thank you for bringing the dog. My response to this is that the dog loves it, and I love it. I tell them, truthfully, that it is a privilege to be allowed to visit, and that the people always make my day. If you ever stop feeling this way about therapy dog visits, reconsider your commitment and decide if you need to make changes. When you love your volunteer job, you have so much more to give to it.

## THE HANDLER IS THE KEY

As facilities and therapy dog organizations consider rules and qualifications, the handler will always be the key. Every therapy dog is entitled to a handler at all times when working.

Therapy dog work happens on the local, personal level. The public recognizes reliable handlers. The staff of every facility eliminates handlers and dogs they don't trust, no matter what certifications they have. Facilities must always have this freedom, and it's the handler's job to earn their confidence.

This book is not intended to frighten people about the risks of therapy dog work. The risks are extremely low. My goal is to help handlers learn to control and protect their dogs, so they put people at ease with skill and courtesy. The best way to protect people and dogs in therapy dog work is to provide each dog with a good handler.

Therapy dog training and handling isn't mysterious. We have the knowledge to take care of the dogs, to condition them to handling, to train them for control, to teach them social skills and to handle them skillfully with people. Life with a trained therapy dog is a life filled with joy and love.

The End

## IF THE DOG IS NOT A REGISTERED THERAPY DOG

This statement would be helpful for facilities to use for owners of visiting dogs that are not registered as therapy dogs:

1. When my dog comes to visit, its coat will be clean and free of tangles.
2. When my dog comes to visit, it will be (a) in good health, (b) free of internal parasites (hookworms, heartworm, coccidiosis, etc.), and (c) free of external parasites (fleas, ticks, mites)
3. My dog will have received all vaccinations, including a rabies vaccination given by a veterinarian. If the dog's vaccinations were not up to date when this series was given, the dog will not visit until two weeks after completing the series of vaccinations, or when the veterinarian says immunization is complete.
4. My dog will be kept under control at all times. The dog will not be permitted to display or act out any aggression toward another animal or person. My dog and I have trained together, and I can completely control my dog. My dog is adequately socialized to people and to other animals. I know an animal can cause serious injury by tripping or scratching people as well as by biting, and I will control my dog to prevent such injuries. I will also protect my dog at all times from abuse, realizing abuse can make a dog dangerous.
5. My dog is housetrained. If there is an accident, I will clean it up and notify the staff so proper disinfectant procedures can be followed. I will take my dog to whatever area the facility designates for dogs to relieve themselves, and I will pick up after my dog in this area also.
6. I have insurance that covers liability if my dog injures anyone.

Signature:_____

# 10

# APPENDICES

## Appendix 1
## Teaching a Therapy Dog Class

Therapy dog classes help new volunteer therapy dog handlers develop the skills to successfully remain in service. Some therapy dog classes will decide to accept dogs and handlers at the beginning of basic control training. Other instructors may want students to have gained those skills in a general dog-training program first.

Screen the dogs and handlers according to your group's criteria before accepting them into class. It will save a lot of wasted class time and handler disappointment later. A tactful leader can explain the health, temperament or training problems that make a particular dog unsuited for class at the current time. Genuine concern for people in these situations can bring valuable volunteers back again when their circumstances are more appropriate. You can find the tests for the major national registries on their websites or by writing to their mailing addresses, both of which are listed in the Resources at the end of this book.

### Therapy Dog Training Begins

Teach students to clean up after their dogs at the class site. If they're not comfortable cleaning up there, they certainly won't be comfortable cleaning up on therapy dog visits.

Therapy dog class is a good place to discuss proper grooming, too. It's not unusual for a dog to come to a training class dirty, with fleas, or with tangled hair. Make students aware of the need to get all this in order before considering therapy dog visits. Since different dogs have different grooming needs, you may need to speak to students about this on an individual basis.

Stays in the Sit, Down and Stand positions are worth the class's time to practice at every meeting. Stays put dogs in quiet, cooperative attitudes, and are incredibly important in therapy dog work. Practicing Stays is a wonderful, nonconfrontational way to put a dog into a calm working mode.

Stays in class provide the opportunity to move wheelchairs, canes, crutches and walkers around the dogs. You'll be able to both observe and improve the dogs' reactions. You can obtain this medical equipment cheaply at thrift stores and garage sales. If a dog has a special problem with any piece of equipment, arranging for the handler to take it home and work with it there for a couple of weeks will usually solve the problem.

Class is a great place for handlers to practice praising and verbally encouraging their dogs in front of other people, and to overcome any remaining self-consciousness. Teach them how to handle their dogs with the appropriate voice tones, physical interventions and collars for therapy dog settings.

### Role-Playing

Role-playing is one of the most valuable uses of class time. Try to recruit volunteers without dogs to play roles. If you must use handlers who have their dogs with them, have the dogs secured before their handlers interact with other people's dogs. Even well trained dogs will break position when their handlers leave them loose on Stays and go act silly with other dogs.

When role-playing, have one handler at a time work a dog with the volunteer, while the instructor coaches and the other handlers watch. If each handler goes through it, they make a sympathetic audience. The negative responses, such as a person afraid or allergic, provide powerful lessons. Handlers learn they must not force their dogs on anyone. They also learn, when they see and hear everyone in the class go through the same situation, not to take personally someone's reluctance to pet their dogs.

Use the role-playing time to help each handler learn to maneuver his or her particular dog into good petting positions for people with various limitations. Set up as many situations as you can over the course of the six weeks, including tight spaces where a dog needs to squeeze between a chair or bed and a wall. If you don't have a bed, try a row of folding chairs with the backs forming a barrier. The petting volunteer can sit in one of the chairs and pet the dog over or under the chair's backrest, which is a pretty fair simulation of the circumstances when a person is in a bed with rails.

Coach the students about safety around walkers and wheelchairs. Specifically, never use "Paws Up" to a walker, which could easily tip with the dog's weight. You can have the dog put Paws Up to your forearm and hold the dog for the person standing with the walker to pet. Take great care not to cause a person to lose their balance. With both wheelchairs and walkers, the person is safest in a straight position or leaning slightly to the side to pet your dog. People can tip right out of a wheelchair by leaning too far forward. If the wheelchair has footrests attached, the dog is limited in how close it can get to them in front, making it a rather long reach for the person to pet the dog. Teach students how to set the brakes on a wheelchair, too.

Encourage everyone in the class to use the mobility equipment and move around with it, dogs at their sides. This is educational for both the dogs and the owners.

I found volunteers in my class shy and at a loss when asked to imitate behaviors we might encounter on therapy dog visits. So I made up the following list. I handed copies of the list out to the volunteers, and let them choose behaviors they felt comfortable playing.

On occasion, include tote bags, floppy hats, overcoats, bathrobes, and similar items for the dogs to experience. Try to get as many types of people as you can, including children and men.

## Assignment Behaviors for "Friendly Stranger" Volunteers

- I am hard of hearing.
- I am hard of hearing and I can't remember the dog's name or the dog's age. I keep asking, over and over.
- I can't move my right arm, and my left arm has spasms and moves involuntarily.
- I walk unsteadily.
- I use a wheelchair.
- I use a cane, walker or crutches.
- I cannot see.
- The only response I make is to move one hand.
- The only response I give is to smile.
- I say, "Get that dog away from me!"
- When I was a child, my father used to kick our family dog whenever it got in his way. The dog would cry. It was the same breed as your dog. I tell this story over and over.
- I am afraid of dogs.
- I am allergic to dogs.
- I start to cry. In a few minutes I work through the tears and begin smiling and enjoying the dog.

## Necessary Skills

Talk to students about constructive conversation on therapy dog visits. Trying to psychoanalyze people we visit is inappropriate. Instead, we can help by encouraging the people to speak positively and to work at their prescribed therapy. Graphic details of our own medical problems are not helpful, either.

Explain proper behavior with a dog on an elevator. When possible, it is preferable for the handler and dog to get on an elevator without other people already on it, so no one is forced into close contact with the dog. It is most polite to move the dog to the back of the elevator and have it sit. If the dog drools on a slick elevator floor, the handler needs to wipe it dry.

Help the students understand facility rules they may encounter. For example, they may be asked not to visit individual rooms because of safety concerns in a psychiatric unit, or infectious disease protocols and roommate concerns in other types of units. In locked Alzheimer's and psychiatric units, they need to exercise caution to help keep people from wandering out with them when they open the door.

In psychiatric units they might see people throwing things, making rough physical movements including grabbing the dog's leash, and having difficulties with self control. The correct procedure is to summon staff, not try to control people yourself. Provide handlers with guidance in class to help them decide what types of facilities best suit them and their dogs.

Therapy dog classes are a joy for experienced volunteers to teach, when handlers and dogs have been screened in advance. Many people will not need a special therapy dog class in order to begin therapy dog visits, but classes seem to increase the numbers of available volunteers.

Following are lesson plans for a six-week therapy dog class, where students and their dogs have passed a Canine Good Citizen Test or evaluation of temperament and basic training as a prerequisite to the class. It is preferable to limit enrollment to five to ten students. The following lesson plan is only an outline; it is important to read the entire preceding text.

## Lesson Plans

### Class One
1. Have handlers and dogs seated in a semi-circle, facing a wheelchair and a few other chairs for the volunteers who will interact with the dogs.

2. Pass out "Assignment Behaviors" sheets, and class homework.

3. Discuss corrections and collars that are acceptable on therapy dog visits (specific to the rules of your organization).

4. Explain why it is important never to correct a therapy dog while it is in the act of being friendly.

5. Have at least three "friendly strangers" set up for interactions, using a wheelchair, cane and walker. Include any other medical equipment available to you. Direct each handler to go to each of the people with his or her dog. Coach each person, while the rest of the group observes. If your group is large, you might have to split into two groups and have an assistant coach part of the students. Make sure one of your "friendly strangers" poses as being for some reason unwilling to have the dog near, and that each student has the opportunity to experience this at every class. Be clear with the students that when a person says "No," this must be respected.

6. Demonstrate how to clean up dog poop with a plastic bag, and explain why it is never appropriate to leave any waste behind at a health care facility.

7. Discuss the difference between precision training and training that encourages a dog to stop and think before acting. Precision training would make a fast adjustment. Training to preserve initiative would give the dog a verbal prompt first, with slower physical repositioning of the dog only if needed after that.

8. Explain that how you handle your dog in public shapes what people think of the dog, and serves as a model for how they will treat your dog. Explain and demonstrate verbal encouragement.

9. Introduce the Stand exercise.

10. Have the group practice a two-minute Sit-Stay and four—minute Down-Stay, with volunteers moving gently around the room using canes and walkers. Coach the volunteers to keep a distance from each dog that helps the dog achieve

success. If any dog is nervous about the equipment, coach that owner in ways to help the dog gradually get used to it. If any dog is not ready for Stays of this duration, coach the handler to time the Stay and release the dog at the appropriate time. Encourage this handler to practice daily at home and in other settings to further the dog's Stay training.

## Class Two

1. With handlers and dogs seated, discuss the pros and cons of treats on therapy dog visits.
2. Introduce the Greeting exercise.
3. Coach the handlers in role-playing with your friendly stranger volunteers, including the Greeting exercise.
4. Have the group practice the Stand exercise, with petting.
5. Seat handlers on the floor around the room, allowing plenty of space between dogs. Demonstrate and discuss cuddling, daily grooming, and socialization outings.
6. Practice Sit-Stays and Down-Stays as in Class One.

## Class Three

1. Start the class with handlers seated in chairs. If a small dog on a platform is available, demonstrate this at the first of the class, and demonstrate how different handlers may use different methods to position their dogs for petting.
2. Practice role-playing with friendly strangers
3. With all handlers standing, demonstrate the Finish from both directions.
4. Review the Stand exercise
5. Practice Sit-Stays and Down-Stays as in Class One, but add brief, gentle touches to the dogs on stays.

## Class Four

1. With handlers and dogs seated, explain how to teach signals, and demonstrate some useful ones, particularly the Come.

2. Explain the difference between a command and a cue. A cue gives the dog the option to refuse.

3. Role-play greetings with the friendly strangers

4. Introduce and coach students on Positions-in-Place: Sit/Down/Stand, two cycles of each, with command and signal given simultaneously for each position.

5. Review Finish, and demonstrate reducing foot movements

6. Sit-Stays and Down-Stays, with medical equipment and soft petting. Remember to keep the situation sufficiently calm that dogs do not feel they must move to get out of the way.

## Class Five

1. With handlers seated, discuss the importance of letting staff and others in the facility know you are there as a volunteer, rather than a paid service provider.

2. Discuss various approaches to people with therapy dogs:
   a. Group visit to 2-12 people, circulating dog and keeping group included in the conversation.
   b. Extroverted, head-on approach: "Do you want to pet my dog?" People might say "No" because:
      1. It's the first choice they have been given about anything all day.
      2. They don't want to monopolize the dog.
      3. They didn't understand the question.
      4. They are embarrassed at being the center of attention.
   c. "Do you like dogs?" "He/She likes to be petted." Model petting.
   d. Quiet, nonverbal approach, reading body language.
   e. Backing the dog up to people who are nervous of the dog's face.
   f. Mix and match.

3. Practice role-playing with the friendly strangers.

4. Introduce and help the students practice "Paws Up." Explain "Come Up" and practice it with a sturdy platform for the dogs.

5. Practice the Finish
6. Practice Positions-in-Place
7. Practice Sit-Stay and Down-Stay with medical equipment and soft touches to the dogs.

## Class Six (Final)

1. With handlers seated, discuss potential accidents and injuries:
   a. Broken skin from tooth or toenail
   b. Bruises from dog's weight on people
   c. Dog feeling pain or fear, including being cornered
   d. Children in the dog's face. Keep your hand on dog, with counter-balancing touches.
   e. Fights or play between dogs, causing bites or falls to people
   f. Dog overly stressed
   g. When someone won't let go of the dog, and other abuse
   h. Dog retrieving for others
   i. Falls:
      1. Water spilled on vinyl or tile floor
      2. Traffic patterns
      3. Frail people standing up or sitting down
      4. Other people taking the dog's leash
      5. Handler not present
   j. Handler inattention
   k. Treats
2. Tell students they need to carry vaccination and insurance papers, and show sincere concern for any injured person. Lawsuits against volunteers are unlikely. Notify your therapy dog registry in the event of an injury. Your dog could be quarantined.
3. Discuss Shake Hands, Kiss, Nose and Head on Lap. Demonstrate training techniques.
4. Role play with friendly strangers
5. Review the Finish
6. Review Positions-in-Place

7. Practice Sit-Stay and Down-Stay

Provide each Student with an Individual Evaluation, including the following:

1. Handler's name:
2. Dog's name:
3. Additional skills practice recommended:
4. Is the dog currently ready for nursing-home visits? (If not, why not?):
5. Is the dog ready for other visits, and if so, what kinds?

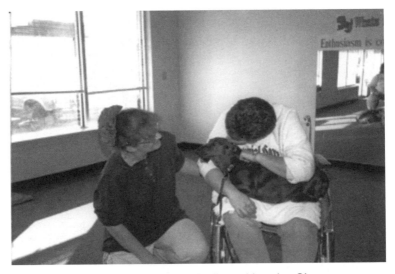

*Therapy dog class helped Kathy Carlin and her dog Sierra prepare for many assignments, including comforting families and rescue workers after the bombing of the Murrah Building in Oklahoma City. Role-playing in therapy dog class as shown here provides handlers with instructor coaching to practice a variety of skills, including the best ways to get their particular dogs close to people for petting. (courtesy of Full Circle)*

# Appendix 2
## Therapy Dogs Resources List

Note: Regional and local testing/registration organizations for therapy dogs are too numerous for us to list them all. Some are affiliated with the national registries, and you can find the ones in your area by contacting the national organizations. Others you can find by contacting local dog obedience training organizations and animal welfare groups. The dog training instructors in your community will usually be able to refer you to the groups actively doing therapy dog visits.

### National Therapy Dog Registries

Delta Society
Pet Partners
289 Perimeter Road East
Renton, WA 98055-1329
(425) 226-7357 (9:00 a.m. - 5:00 p.m. PST, Monday - Friday)
(425) 235-1076 (fax)
Email: info@deltasociety.org
Website: www.deltasociety.org

Therapy Dogs International, Inc.
88 Bartley Road
Flanders, NJ 07836
(973) 252-9800
(973) 252-7171 (fax)
Email: tdi@gti.net
Website: www.tdi-dog.org

Therapy Dogs, Inc.
P.O. Box 5868
Cheyenne, WY 82003
(877) 843-7364
(307) 638-2079 (fax)
Email: therdog@sisna.com
Website: www.therapydogs.com

The St. John's Ambulance Therapy Dogs (Canada)
St. John Ambulance Halton Hills
P.O. Box 145, Norval
Ontario, Canada
L0P 1K0
(905) 873-8442
(905) 873-7646 (fax)
Email: brigade@sja-haltonhills.org
Website: www.sja-haltonhills.org/brigade.html

## Human/Animal Bond Informational Resources
The Latham Foundation
Latham Plaza Bld.
1826 Clement Avenue
Alameda, CA 95401
(510) 521-0920
(510) 521-9861 (fax)
Email: info@Latham.org
Website: www.latham.org

The San Francisco SPCA
2500-16th Street
San Francisco, CA 94103-4213
(415) 554-3000
(415) 552-7041 (fax)
E-mail: publicinfo@sfspca.org
Website: www.sfspca.org

## Internet Information Resources
www.dog-play.com
Dog Play.

www.cofc.edu/~huntc/service.html
Professor Hunt's Dog Page.

www.vin.com
Veterinary Information Network, for veterinarians.

www.petcareforum.com
Pet Care Forum, with message boards, chat rooms, and other resources—including the Canine Behavior Series with questions answered by Kathy Diamond Davis.

www.inch.com/~dogs
American Dog Trainers Network.

www.clickerlessons.com
Greenwood Dog Training School's site, Clicker Training Lessons to do-it-yourself.

www.volhard.com
Jack and Wendy Volhard, Trainers of Trainers.

www.petsandpeople.org
Pets and People, Companions in Therapy and Service.

## Resources for Information about Assistance Dogs for People with Disabilities

Assistance Dogs International
www.assistance-dogs-intl.org

International Association of Assistance Dog Partners
Editor/Information and Advocacy Center
38691 Filly Drive
Sterling Heights, MI 48310
(586) 826-3938
Email: info@iaadp.org
Website: www.iaadp.org

### National Dog Trainer Organizations

Association of Pet Dog Trainers
1-800-PET-DOGS
Email: information@apdt.com
Website: www.apdt.com

National Association of Dog Obedience Instructors
(NADOI)
Attn: Corresponding Secretary
PMB #369
729 Grapevine Hwy, Suite 369
Hurst, TX 76054-2085
Website: www.nadoi.org

International Association of Canine Professionals
P.O. Box 560156
Monverde, FL 34756-0156
(407) 469-2008
(407) 469-7127
Email: iacp@mindspring.com
Website: www.dogpro.org

### Dog Books

Dogwise
P.O. Box 2778
Wenatchee, WA 98807-2778
Orders: 1-800-776-2665
Direct: 1-509-663-9115
FAX: 1-509-662-7233
Email: mail@dogwise.com
Website: www.dogwise.com
Your best source for books on dogs, plus some nifty treats
and toys.

Dog Lovers Bookshop
P.O. Box 117
Gracie Station
New York, NY 10028
(212) 369-7554 (phone and fax)
Email: info@dogbooks.com
Website: www.dogbooks.com
A great source for out-of-print dog books.

AKC Headquarters
260 Madison Avenue
New York, NY 10016
(212) 696-8200
Website: www.akc.org
The AKC can help you to locate the AKC-affiliated clubs nearest you for training classes, find information on the Canine Good Citizen Test, and to contact reputable breeders and rescue workers involved with each AKC-registered breed.

**Temperament Testing**
American Temperament Test Society, Inc.
P.O. Box 4093
St Louis, MO 63136
(314) 869-6103
Email: info@atts.org
Website: www.atts.org

**Equipment and Supplies**
Dogwise - books, videos, toys, training, tools, treats
701 B Poplar
P.O. Box 2778
Wenatchee, WA 98807-2778
Orders: 1-800-776-2665
Direct: 1-509-663-9115
FAX: 1-509-662-7233
Email: mail@dogwise.com
Website: www.dogwise.com

Nordkyn Outfitters - nylon webbing, harnesses and collars
P.O. Box 1023
Graham, WA 98338
(253) 847-4128
(253) 847-4108 (fax)
Orders Only: 1-800-326-4128
Email: nordkyn@nordkyn.com
Website: www.nordkyn.com

Drs. Foster & Smith - all sorts of dog products
2353 Air Park Road
P.O. Box 100
Rhinelander, WI  54501-0100
Orders: 1-800-826-7206
Email: CustomerService@DrsFosterSmith.com
Website: www.DrsFosterSmith.com

Handcraft Collars - quality nylon collars that don't stretch
out of size
4875 Camp Creek Road
Pell City, AL 35125
(800) 837-2033
(205) 338-0439 (fax)
Email: Handcraft1@aol.com
Website: www.handcraftcollars.com

J and J Dog Supplies - competition dog training equipment
P.O. Box 1517
Galesburg, IL 61402-1517
(800) 642-2050
(309) 344-3522 (fax)
Email: mail@jandjdog.com
Website: www.jandjdog.com

J – B Wholesale Pet Supplies - general pet supplies
5 Raritan Road
Oakland, NJ 07436
Orders: (800) 526-0388
FAX: (800) 788-5005
Email: jbpet@intac.com
Website: www.jbpet.com

The Dog's Outfitter
Humboldt Industrial Park
1 Maplewood Drive
Hazleton, PA 18201-9798
(800) 367-3647
(570) 384-4843 (fax)
Email: customerservice@dogsoutfitter.com
Website: www.dogsoutfitter.com

Care-a-Lot
1617 Diamond Springs Road
Virginia Beach, VA 23455
(800) 343-7680
(757) 460-9771 (local)
(757) 460-0317 (fax)
Email: customerservice@carealotpets.com
Website: www.carealotpets.com

**Dog Magazines**
AKC Gazette
4th Floor
260 Madison Avenue
New York, NY 10016
(800) 533-7323 (subscriptions)
Website: www.akc.org

Dog Fancy
P.O. Box 53264
Boulder, CO 80322-3264
(800) 365-4421
(303) 604-7455 (fax)
Email: fancy@neodata.com
Website: www.dogfancy.com

Dog World
500 North Dearborn, Suite 1100
Chicago, IL 60610
(312) 396-0600
(312) 467-7118 (fax)
Email: dogworld3@aol.com
Website: www.dogworldmag.com

OffLead
6 State Road, #113
Mechanicsburg, PA 17050
(717) 691-3388
(717) 691-3381 (fax)
Email: offlead3@aol.com
Website: www.off-lead.com

## Contact the Author

Kathy Diamond Davis
4425 NW 52nd St.
Oklahoma City, OK 73112-2115
(405) 947-5413
Email: KDiamondD@aol.com

# Appendix 3
## Therapy Dogs Annotated Bibliography

Anderson, Moira, M.Ed. *Coping with Sorrow on the Loss of Your Pet*, copyright 1994. Therapy dog handlers regularly encounter people grieving the loss of a dog. This book will help prepare you to benefit the people you encounter who are feeling this pain. It will also help you when you lose your therapy dog, which is, sadly, inevitable, unless your dog happens to outlive you.

Baer, Ted. *Communicating with Your Dog*, copyright 1989. Movie work with dogs, tricks. As with therapy dogs, this training requires that you maintain in your dog the ability to be able to learn/understand to do the task differently, when the situation is different.

Bryson, Sandy. *Search Dog Training*, copyright 1984. If you can't find this one, read other books on Search and Rescue dog training. Like therapy dogs, these dogs need to work well with the public, and they are trained in ways that preserve their initiative. Reading about this training will undoubtedly expand your understanding of the canine mind.

Burch, Mary R., Ph.D. *Volunteering With Your Pet: How to Get Involved in Animal-Assisted Therapy With Any Kind of Pet*, copyright 1996. Written by one of the most respected people in the field, this book includes safety information, ideas, and goals for using animals (not just dogs) in therapeutic interactions.

Burch, Mary R., Ph.D. and Bailey, Jon S., Ph.D. *How Dogs Learn*, copyright 1999. Information every dog handler needs to understand.

Burnham, Patricia Gail. *Playtraining Your Dog*, copyright 1980. Some of the best of competition training from the past.

Butler, Beverly. *Maggie By My Side*, copyright 1987. Butler lost her eyesight at age 14, and this is the account of her partnership with her fifth guide dog.

Cairns, Julie. *The Golden Retriever: All That Glitters*, copyright 1999. A breed born for therapy dog work, and a book exactly right to help prospective owners.

Campbell, William E. *Behavior Problems in Dogs*, copyright 1992 (or more recent edition). Great dog behavior information from an expert who continues to refine his knowledge and methods.

Coile, D. Caroline. *German Shepherds for Dummies*, copyright 2000. An outstanding contribution to the literature on this incredible breed that includes therapy dog work among its many abilities. The first dog registered with Therapy Dogs International was a GSD.

Colflesh, Linda. *Making Friends: Training Your Dog Positively*, copyright 1990. Good training info, for the most part. My favorite quote, though, is not about training. Colflesh writes, "My husband...chose a Belgian Tervuren, a breed that is not readily recognized and in fact is often mistaken for a Collie-Shepherd mix. This reflects his distaste for displays of wealth." Very perceptive comment on the variety of reasons people choose particular breeds. (Out of Print)

Coren, Stanley. *The Intelligence of Dogs*, copyright 1994. Explains exactly what went into that determination of the Border Collie as "the most intelligent breed," the limitations of our understanding of any dog's intelligence, why intelligent dogs are not easy dogs to handle, and how to test your own dog's intelligence.

Cusack, Odean and Smith, Elaine. *Pets and the Elderly: The Therapeutic Bond*, copyright 1984. Elaine Smith founded Therapy Dogs International. A wealth of early scientific information and references about the use of animals in health-care settings. (Hard to find.)

Davis, Joel. *With Alex by My Side*, copyright 2000. Insights into life with an assistance dog.

Davis, Kathy Diamond, *Responsible Dog Ownership*, copyright 1994. Covers issues of dog selection, care and management that are outside the scope of this book, but essential for therapy dog handlers to understand. (Out of Print)

Delta Society. *Pet Partners Volunteer Training Manual.* Essential if you wish to register your dog as a Pet Partner. The Delta Society is also a source for a vast amount of other material—print and video—related to animals in therapeutic settings, including scientific research in the field. See the Resources list for Delta Society contact information.

Dodman, Nicholas, BVMS, MRCVS. *The Dog Who Loved Too Much: Tales, Treatments and the Psychology of Dogs,* copyright 1996. Written by one of the world's leading veterinary specialists in dog behavior.

Eames, Ed and Toni. *Partners in Independence: A Success Story of Dogs and the Disabled,* copyright 1997. How dogs assist people who have disabilities, the legal rights of people with disabilities with their assistance dogs, and other valuable information for anyone interested in this area. The book "A Guide to Guide Dog Schools," by the same authors, will help anyone with a disability to consider the choices available when seeking an assistance dog.

Fogle, Bruce, D.V.M. *Know Your Dog: An Owner's Guide to Dog Behavior,* copyright 1992. Photographs and explanations of dog behavior and body language.

Gibbs, Margaret. *Leader Dogs for the Blind: 'For Whither Thou Goest',* copyright 1982. I will always treasure this book for Gibbs' information on how to preserve and build initiative in a working dog.

Giffin, James M., MD and Carlson, Lisa D., DVM. *Dog Owner's Home Veterinary Handbook,* Third Edition, copyright 2000. Excellent resource for any dog owner, especially a therapy dog handler.

Haggarty, Capt. Arthur J. *How to Get Your Pet Into Show Business,* copyright 1994, and *How to Teach Your Dog to Talk (and Other Tricks),* copyright 2000. If you're interested in the entertainment aspects of dog training, whether for fun or profit, these books contain a wealth of information and ideas.

Haggarty, Capt. Arthur J., and Benjamin, Carol Lea. *Dog Tricks: Training Your Dog to be Useful, Fun, and Entertaining,* copyright 1978. Some of the training methods are tough, but the book contains loads of trick ideas(Out of Print).

Hart, Benjamin L., D.V.M., Ph.D. and Hart, Lynette A., Ph.D., *The Perfect Puppy: How to Choose Your Dog by Its Behavior*, copyright 1988. Explains differences among 56 different breeds.

Herriot, James. *James Herriot's Dog Stories*, copyright 1986. Perfect as an adjunct to therapy dog visits. Recommend it to healthcare facilities as something they can do between visits.

Hickford, Jessie. *Eyes at My Feet*, copyright 1973. Vivid picture of life with a guide dog, written by a former English teacher who trained with her first guide dog after losing her eyesight at age 52.

Hodgson, Sarah. *Dog Tricks for Dummies*, copyright 2000. Therapy dog visits can be enhanced by tricks, and this book is loaded with ideas.

Hoffman, Martha. *Lend Me an Ear: The Temperament, Selection and Training of the Hearing Dog*, copyright 1999. Practical information about hearing dogs, and useful insights for therapy dogs.

Humphrey, Elliott and Warner, Lucien. *Working Dogs: An Attempt to Produce a Strain of German Shepherds Which Combines Working Ability and Beauty of Conformation*, copyright 1934. Came out of the work done in Switzerland, at Fortunate Fields, which among other achievements, led to the establishment of the guide dog training school in the U.S., The Seeing Eye, Inc (Out of Print).

Kilcommons, Brian with Wilson, Sarah. *Good Owners, Great Dogs*, copyright 1992. Astute perceptions about dogs, from a masterful communicator.

Livingood, Lee. *Retired Racing Greyhounds for Dummies*, copyright 2000. These dogs are being extensively used in therapy dog work, and Livingood understands both the dogs and how to train them.

Lorenz, Konrad. *Man Meets Dog*, copyright 1953. Valuable insights about dog behavior and what dog's lives were like in the past.

Lorenz, Konrad. *On Aggression*, copyright 1963. The nature of aggression in all creatures.

Levorsen, Bella. *Mush! A Beginner's Manual of Sled Dog Training*, copyright 1976. Aids understanding of sled-dog breeds, and of training that preserves initiative.

McCaig, Donald. *Nop's Trials*, copyright 1984. Excellent book to help you understand your sheep-herding breed's thinking.

McKinney, Betty Jo and Hagen-Rieseberg, Barbara. *Sheltie Talk*, copyright 1985. Incredible insights into the world of conformation showing and breeding, plus a definitive text on a breed that excels in therapy dog work.

Milani, Myrna M, D.V.M.. *The Body Language and Emotion of Dogs*, copyright 1986. Helps readers not only understand their dogs, but their own, sometimes-inappropriate reactions to dog behavior.

Montagu, Ashley. *Touching: The Human Significance of the Skin*, Third Edition, copyright 1996. Touching is a part of therapy dog work: people touching your dog, and touch from your dog or from you to a person. This book will give you a wealth of insight into how touch affects people, and perhaps a bit of how it affects dogs, too.

Morn, September. *Dogs Love to Please…We Teach Them How!* copyright 1992. Good relationship-building training. (Hard to find.)

Morris, Desmond. *Dogwatching*, copyright 1986. The author's stated purpose: "to demonstrate that we can learn about dogs by direct observation and by observational experiments, WITHOUT HARMING THEM." A short book with many insights into dog behavior.

Nordensson, Stewart and Kelley, Lydia. *Teamwork for People with Disabilities*, Volumes One and Two, copyright 1997. Loaded with dog training ideas for people who have physical limitations. Inspiring.

Ogden, Paul. *Chelsea: The Story of a Signal Dog*, copyright 1992. A Belgian Sheepdog trained by Canine Companions for Independence as assistant to a man with hearing impairment (Out of Print).

Project BREED. *Breed Rescue Efforts and Education Directory Series*, Volumes One and Two, copyright 1989, 1993. This network did magnificent work rescuing dogs before every AKC breed had a rescue organization. If you can get your hands on these books, they include profile information on many breeds, with the difficulties rescuers might encounter in each breed (health and behavior), often not found in breed books.

Pryor, Karen. *Don't Shoot the Dog!*, copyright 1984 (or later edition). A must, to gain understanding of how to apply positive reinforcement. Read it more than once!

Randolph, Mary. *Dog Law*, copyright 1988. A topic every dog owner and particularly every therapy dog handler needs to understand.

Rutherford, Clarice and Neil, David M., M.R.C.V.S. *How to Raise a Puppy You Can Live With*, newest edition is 2001. A classic.

Ryan, Terry and Shipp, Theresa, Editors, *The Ultimate Puppy*, copyright 2001. Excellent resource for puppy raising, training, socializing, and health care. Stunning color photographs.

Spadafori, Gina. *Dogs for Dummies*, Second Edition, copyright 2001. Frank talk about what to expect from various types of dogs and responsible dog management.

Taggart, Mari. *Sheepdog Training: an All-Breed Approach*, copyright 1986. How are herding dogs trained, what tasks do they learn to perform, and how do the different herding breeds vary from one another? If you have an interest in doing therapy dog work with a herding-breed dog, this book will help you to understand how your dog thinks (Out of Print).

Tarrant, Bill. *Training the Hunting Retriever*, copyright 1991. To understand a Labrador, read about the work the breed was originally bred to do. Tarrant was not only a wonderful writer, he was also a wonderful dog man. Quote: "You can take the spirit out of a pup, but you can't put it back in." Also look for his *Hey Pup, Fetch It Up!* copyright 1993, and *The Magic of Dogs*, copyright 1995.

Tucker, Michael. *Solving Your Dog Problems*, copyright 1987; *Dog Training Made Easy*, copyright 1980; and *Dog Training Step by Step: A New Guide for Owners and Instructors*, copyright 1991. An outstanding trainer and instructor with an extensive background in guide dog training and in training owners with their companion dogs. Major experience with German Shepherd Dogs and Labradors (Out of Print).

Tucker, Michael. *The Eyes That Lead: The Story of Guide Dogs for the Blind*, copyright 1984. Great ideas for building the ability of a dog to work in public. Explains the use of verbal encouragement, and other intricate details of guide dog training (Out of Print).

Volhard, Jack and Wendy. *The Canine Good Citizen*, copyright 1994. Valuable information on canine drives as well as effective and humane training appropriate for therapy dogs.

Volhard, Jack and Wendy. *Dog Training for Dummies*, copyright 2001. Incorporates much information from their other books, including the excellent, *Open and Utility Training: The Motivational Method*. Their philosophy is to train for early success and frequent success. Elegant methods that yield happy, reliably trained dogs. Their videos are wonderfully instructive, too.

Volhard, Wendy. *Holistic Guide for a Healthy Dog*, Second Edition, copyright 2000. Overview of a myriad of alternative options for your dog's care.

Walkowicz, Chris. *Choosing a Dog for Dummies*, copyright 2001. Help for people trying to narrow down their choices of a breed or mix to adopt. Includes brief profile information for about 150 breeds.

Walton, Joel and Adamson, Eve. *Labrador Retrievers for Dummies*, copyright 2000. Includes good information on teaching safe habits to dogs and children so they can live together in peace. Strong position against training that uses any form of correction.

Weiss, Lisa and Biegel, Emily. *The Labrador Retriever: The Dog That Does It All*, copyright 1999. The most numerous breed in AKC registrations, the Labrador is also an outstanding choice for both assistance dog work and therapy dog work. This book focuses on breedings intended for conformation and guide dog functions, rather than on the lines bred more for hunting. Excellent to read before choosing a Labrador partner for therapy dog work.

White, Betty and Sullivan, Tom *The Leading Lady: Dinah's Story*, copyright 1991. Tom Sullivan's guide dog experience. Sometimes while reading this book, I wanted to throttle him for thoughtless treatment of his dog! (Hard to find.)

Wilcox, Bonnie, D.V.M., and Walkowicz, Chris. *Old Dogs, Old Friends: Enjoying Your Older Dog*, copyright 1991. Therapy dogs often grow old in the job, and certainly grow old in their handlers' homes. Great help here for making the most of this wonderful stage of your dog's life. (Hard to find.)

Wilson, Cindy C., and Turner, Dennis C. *Companion Animals in Human Health*, copyright 1998. Theories, methodologies and conclusions of scientific research on how HIA (Human-Animal Interaction) affects human QL (Quality of Life). Such research may influence expenditures of future health-care dollars as well as public social policies.

Wood, Deborah. *Help for Your Shy Dog*, copyright 1999. Outstanding not only for someone with a seriously shy dog, but for anyone wanting to understand how to build healthy confidence in a dog, especially a sensitive one.

Woodhouse, Barbara. *No Bad Dogs: The Woodhouse Way*, copyright 1978, 1982. If you ever get a chance to watch her old television show, don't miss it. Watch her TIMING. Some of the ideas in the book are odd, but mixed in are brilliant insights. It was from her I got the idea to teach my therapy dogs to move toward people and greet them. She called it "Go and Talk." Brian Kilcommons did some of his early training with Woodhouse.

Yates, Elizabeth. *Sound Friendships*, copyright 1987. Combines a heart-warming story with information about a program that trains dogs to aid people who have impaired hearing.

Zielinski, Stan. *Saint Bernards from the Stoan Perspective*, copyright 1999. An incredible book about dog breeding at its best.

# Appendix 4
# Fun Stuff

### Therapy Dog Cards

When I had been involved with therapy dog visits for a few years, I began collecting, and eventually carving, rubber art stamps. Since around 1989, I have made cards with my stamps to give out to the people I visit. The cards serve the purpose of letting staff and family members know who saw the dog on a particular visit, since I bring a different card design each time. The people enjoy the cards, and some collect them. If a person is confused and thinks I'm asking for a donation or selling something with the card, they easily understand my explanation: "It's just for fun!"

### Photographs

On many occasions, I've toted along my camera and shot pictures of folks with the therapy dog. Later I've brought prints of those pictures back to be distributed to the people. This is expensive, and also difficult, since some or all of the people may be gone on your next visit.

A better way to do it is to use instant film when it is available to you. This also resolves any concerns about people's privacy, since you hand them the photograph and there are no negatives or copies. I have visited a few facilities that occasionally have a camera and film available for this, and the people absolutely love it.

### Reward Toy

All of my dogs have enjoyed tennis balls, but tennis balls roll and bounce out of control, making them difficult to use safely in some settings. A few years ago, tennis ball toys with leather straps attached became popular. Now you can buy tennis balls with various things threaded or fastened to them that will work for tossing to your dog's mouth as a special reward or a tension reliever on a therapy dog visit. If your dog prefers another special toy, by all means tote that along and use it, provided it is soft.

Recently I got the idea of making an even more controllable toy. All I had to do was make my usual tennis ball toy with a rope through it, except make the rope longer and the loop smaller. I put the loop around my right thumb and toss the ball to the dog's mouth. I keep hold of the rope, so the dog catches the ball and enjoys it without the ball ever hitting the floor.

This is not a good toy for retrieving games on a therapy dog visit, because the longer rope could get caught on things. The ball with the short rope through it is great for that. But for rewarding a dog in such a way that I keep the attention coming back to my face, the ball with the longer rope is a nice option. It works in situations where I don't have much room, and the fact that I never have to bend over to pick it up is a plus with my arthritis.

### About the Author

Kathy Diamond Davis has been a therapy dog handler since 1985. She has owned, trained and handled five registered therapy dogs in a wide variety of facility settings. Her dog-training experience includes competition obedience and tracking. She wrote a curriculum and taught a therapy dog class for two years.

Kathy has written extensively on the subject of therapy dogs, and is always happy to answer questions from anyone who wishes to email, send a letter, or telephone about therapy dog work.

She responds to questions from dog owners around the world through the Canine Behavior Series of the Pet Care Forum sponsored by the Veterinary Information Network (www.petcareforum.com).

Club affiliations include the Oklahoma City Obedience Training Club, the American Belgian Tervuren Club, and Best Friends of the Oklahoma City Animal Welfare Division.

Education includes a B.A. in English and several college courses in psychology and sociology.

Kathy is a member of the Dog Writers Association of America. She has written for various magazines, including Dog Fancy, Off-Lead, Alpha Affiliates, and Rubberstampmadness. Her book Responsible Dog Ownership was a finalist for the DWAA General Reference Books award.

*Author with Spirit, Believer, and Gabriel.*

# INDEX

**A**

access rights, 4, 36
accidents
dealing with, 57
dog bites, 199–200
safety precautions against, 195–200
treats, 171–73
wet floors, 190
aggressiveness in dogs
male dogs, 25
temperament evaluation, 55, 143
aggressive people, 198–99, 203
allergy concerns, 74
Alzheimer's Disease, 8, 67
class discussion of, 223
conversation skills and, 215
visit interactions, intensity of, 48
American Kennel Club (AKC), 24, 235
Americans with Disabilities Act, 4
American Temperament Test Society, 233
animal-assisted therapy, 4
animals, uncontrolled, 53–55, 64–65
animal shelters, 29
around-behind Finish, 177–80
arthritis (in dogs), 209–10
assistance dogs, 4, 36, 231
attention-deficit problems, 8, 67
Attention-Release training, 55, 90–92, 135

**B**

Back command, 175–76
ball toys, making, 97, 246
barking, 207–8
behaviors, redirecting undesirable, 103, 212

benefits, therapeutic. *See* therapeutic benefits
bite inhibition, 89
seal it with a kiss technique, 103, 104
teaching, 100–103
body language
communication and, 12–14
handler-dog communication, 80–81
of handler in corrections, 108, 110
"reading" people, 155–60, 202–3
of therapy dogs, 34
breed considerations. *See* dogs, choosing a partner
breeders, 24, 26–28
breed rescue groups, 29
breed specific restrictions, 24
buckle collars, 138
burnout
in dog, 193–94
handler, 20, 217

**C**

canes, working around, 220
*Canine Good Citizen, The* , 117, 132
care facilities
breed specific restrictions, 24
facility requirements, 49
facility requirements, working with, 66, 75–76
standards of service, 55–56, 63
statement of responsibility, 218
visitation options, 47–50, 69, 192–93
when to say no, 187–89
children
and dogs' tails, 89–90
face-to-face encounters, 203
safety precautions, 198

socialization to dogs, 15–16, 36–37
teasing dogs, 104
working with, 47–48, 73–75
classes, 219–28
basic training, 220
lesson plans, 223–28
screening for, 219
cleanliness of dog. *See* grooming
Close Your Mouth command, 100, 102–3
collars, types of, 138–39
Come command, 123–27
hand signal, 168
Come Up command, 170–71
commands
Attention-Release, 90–92
Close Your Mouth, 100, 102–3
Come, 123–27
Down-Stay, 83
Finish position, 177–80
Fix It, 110
Front position, 177
Give, 94, 96
Heel, 135–38
Hold It, 93–96
Kiss, 103
Leave It, 110–11
No, variations on, 110
Out, 96
Paws Up, 170–71, 208, 209, 210, 221
Sit-Stay, 127–32
Stand, 140–43
Stay, 83–85
Take It, 93–96
*See also* control work; hand signals; training: issues concerning
commands: issues involving
dog's name, 181
"dynamics" of, 181–82
in foreign languages, 180
ignoring inappropriate, 152–53
for walking skills, 175–76
communication
body language, 12–14
conversation, options for, 213–17, 222
dog language, 114
"dynamics" and tone of voice, 125, 134, 181–82
handler-dog bond, 153–55, 163

language and the spoken word, 180–82
nonverbal, 12–14, 59
use of space in, 204–6
community benefits, 36–37, 160
competition conflicts, therapy work and
handler commitment issues, 33–35, 182–83
training techniques, contrast in, 92, 117–18, 123, 137
complaints, 65
confidentiality agreements, 216
control work, 117–46
Attention training, 90–92
benefits of training, 146
Down-Stay, 132–34
and grooming, 80
and handler abilities, 54–55
hand signals, 164–71
heeling, 135–38
humane training, 118–19
leash use, 76–77
length of training sessions, 123
out-of-sight training, 134
positions-in-place training, 176–77
practice through games, 88–89
public safety, 148–50, 163
recall training, 123–27
retrieving and, 93–96
Sit-Stay, 127–32
Stand, 140–43
stillness, 85
and teasing, 104–5
testing reliability, 124, 149
and trainability, 29
tug-of-war games, 98–99
walking skills, 175–76
*See also* commands; hand signals; training: issues concerning
conversation, options for, 213–17, 222
cooperation
facility staff and residents, 9, 10, 12, 17
between therapys groups, 60–61
correction-reward ratio, 111
corrections
careful use of, 108–11
correction sound, 111
"dynamics" and tone of voice, 125, 134, 181–82
No, variations on, 110

repetition as correction, 109, 154
and Stay command, 131
training hand signals, 167
when not to use, 122, 143, 156
costumes, 191–92
crutches, working around, 220
Cuddle cue, 145
cuddling sessions, 112–15
cues
for greeting, 143–45
subtlety of control, 180
walking skills, 175–76

## D

death encounters, 214
defense drive, 26
disaster work, credentials for, 50–51
disoriented people, 198–99
dog books, sources for, 232–33
dog education programs, 49
dog fights, 54
dog language, 114
dogs, choosing a partner, 23–29
breed considerations, 23–24
employment needed, 30–31
health problems, 26
puppies, 26–28
research resources, 24
sex, 25–26
size, 25
sources for adult dogs, 28–29
unsuitable candidates, 27–28
dog-to-dog encounters
competion for attention, 112–15
dog fights, 54
resident animals, 48–49, 61, 196
uncontrolled animals, 53–55, 64–65
*Dog Training for Dummies*, 95, 117, 132
Down command, 132–34, 142
hand signals, 166–67
Down-Stay command, 83, 132–34
class practice, 220
long stays, 130
for petting, 140–43
drives, Volhard theory of, 117–18

## E

Easy command, 175

equipment and supplies, sources for, 233–35
evaluation standards, 23, 29, 51
dog aggression, 54–55
handler assessment, 44
screening for classes, 219
unsuitable candidates, 27–28

## F

face-to-face encounters
safety concerns, 113–14
territorial ranges, 203
facilities. *See* care facilities
falls, safety precautions against, 196–97
fear period (in children), 74–75
feces, 40–41, 212
feet, touch conditioning of, 173–74
FEMA, disaster work credentials, 50
female dogs, 25–26
Finish position, 177–80
Fix It command, 110
fleas, 40, 201
flooring surfaces
exposure to, 39
older dogs and, 210
food
giving safely, 171–73
as lure in greeting, 144
as motivation in training, 79, 90–91, 135, 140
on visits, 198
friendly attitude (in therapy dogs), 122
"Friendly Stranger" in class practice, 222
Front position, 177

## G

games
retrieving, 92–98
as training tool, 88–89
tug-of-war, 98–99
Give command, 94, 96
goals of, 60, 70–71
Go Out command, hand signals for, 168–69
Go Say Hi, hand signals for, 168–69
Go Through command, 175–76
greeting skills, 143–45, 173–75

grooming, 80, 89
  cleanliness and parasite control,
    40–41
  daily cuddles, 112–15
  health care, 41–44
  tails, 89
  toenails, 197
group cooperation, benefits of, 60–
  61
group visits, 47–62
  approaching people, 71–73
  benefits of joining, 50, 51–53,
    61–62
  evaluation of handler-dog team,
    53
  practice sessions, 51–52
  referrals for one-dog visits, 64
  session length, 67–68, 193–94
  session location, choosing, 68–70
  standards of service, 55–56, 63
  working with children, 47–48
  *See also* one-dog visits; visits,
    aspects of

**H**

handler commitment
  competition conflicts, therapy
    work and, 33–35
  depression, overcoming, 10, 17–
    18
  emotional stress on handler, 48,
    53, 187
  preparation for visits, 186–87
  standards of service, 55–56, 63
  when to say no, 187–89
handler-dog team, 5
  body language communications,
    80–81
  changes in routine of, 70–71
  clothing, 191
  cuddling sessions, 112–15
  and disease transmission, 200–
    201
  dog language communication,
    114
  evaluation of by instructors, 53
  handler as leader, 153
  language and the spoken word,
    180–82
  mental leash between, 77
  new experiences, exposure to, 39,
    105–8, 209, 220

as partnership, 25, 30, 82, 107–8,
  153–55
and positive touch, 84–85
social skills and public relations,
  147–62
stress from overworking, 193–94
handler skills
  attentiveness to dogs, 54–55
  class practice, 220–28
  controlling play, 88–89
  control work and, 29
  corrections, careful use of, 111
  cuddling sessions, 112–15
  handler as interpreter, 211–13
  instructor, choosing, 119–21
  lifting dogs, 85–87
  personal assessment, 44
  placement of dogs on visits,
    205–6
  practicing at veterinary clinic,
    41–43
  protection of dogs, 47, 48, 188–
    89, 195–200, 203–4
  public courtesy, 157–60
  "reading" people, 155–56
  tails, awareness of, 89–90
  understanding territorial ranges,
    202–11
  undesirable behavior, redirecting,
    103, 212
  voice control, 180–82
handling, conditioning dogs to, 79–
  115
  and bite inhibition, 100–103
  car rides, 105
  corrections, careful use of, 108–
    11
  cuddling sessions, 112–15
  of ears, 92
  feet, 173–74
  games, 88–90, 92–99, 104–5
  grooming, 80, 89
  lifting dogs, skill of, 85–87
  of mouth, 95
  new experiences, exposure to,
    105–8
  retrieving, 92–98
  stillness, and Stay command, 83–
    85
  of tails, 89–90
  touch, 14, 79, 80
hand signals, 164–71
  Close Your Mouth, 102
  Come, 168

Down, 132–34, 166–67
Go Out, 168–69
Heel, 167–68
Paws Up, 170–71
Sit, 164–65
Sit command, 129
Stand command, 140
Stay command, 128, 129
Take It, 168–69
vision in aging dogs, 167
*See also* commands; control work
harnesses, 138, 192
head halters, 139, 140
Head on Lap command, 173–75
health care
    and disease transmission, 200–201
    parasite control, 40–41
    veterinarian, relationship with, 41–44
    *See also* grooming
heat cycles, 25
Heel command, 135–38, 197
    Finish position, 177–80
    hand signal, 167–68
high drive, 118
Hold It command, 93–96
homeowners insurance, breed specific restrictions, 24
home visits, potential concerns, 48–49
human/animal bond informational resources, 230
humane training, 118–19

**I**

identification tags, 191
inappropriate commands, ignoring, 152–53
indoor visits, 59
initiative (in therapy dogs), 13–14, 121–22, 153–55
injuries
    to dog when retrieving, 97–98
    safety precautions against, 195–200
insurance
    homeowners, and breed specific restrictions, 24
    liability, 199–200
    through registry organizations, 56
intelligent disobedience, 121–22

internet information resources, 230–31

**J**

"jolly talk", as encouragement, 106
jumping, no-jumping rule, 145, 170

**K**

Kiss command, 103, 173–75

**L**

language, and the spoken word, 180–82
leash handling, 197
    control on visits, 76–77
    Finish position, 177–80
    heeling, 137–38
Leave It command, 110–11
lesson plans, therapy dog classes, 223–28
liability issues
    dog bites, 199–200
    paid professionals and, 37–38
licking, 213
lifting dogs, skill of, 85–87
limited-slip collars, 138
long line, as training tool, 125–26, 131

**M**

male dogs, 25–26
media coverage, 38–39, 47, 184
meeting area visits, 68–70
mental leash, 77
mixed breeds. *See* dogs, choosing a partner
mobility equipment, working around, 72, 209, 220, 221
mouth, handling of dog's, 95
mouthing. *See* bite inhibition
Move command, 175–76

**N**

national dog trainer organizations, 232
national registry organizations, 3–4
    address listings, 229–30
    benefits of joining, 50, 51–53, 61–62

evaluation standards, 23, 29, 51
insurance, 51, 56
registration identification, 57,
  201
neutering, and therapy work, 25–
  26, 43
new experiences, exposure to, 105–
  8
nicknames (of dogs), 180, 182
No command, variations on, 110
no-jumping rule, 145, 170
nonverbal communication, 12–14,
  59
Nose command, 173–75

**O**

obedience training
  choosing an instructor, guidelines
    on, 119–21
  competition conflicts, therapy
    work and, 33–35
  training techniques, contrast in,
    92, 117–18, 123, 137
off-leash control, 29, 76–77
  heeling, 137
  out-of-sight work, 134
  recall training, 126–27
  training Stay, 131–32
Okay command, 91
one-dog visits, 63–77
  approaching people, 71–73
  children, working with, 73–75
  facilities, deciding on, 75–76
  and group experience, 64–65
  scheduling, 66
  session length, 63, 67–68, 193–94
  session location, choosing, 68–70
  staff support on, 65–66
  standards of service, 55–56, 63
  See also group visits; visits,
    aspects of
Out command, 96
outdoor visits, 59
out-of-sight work, training, 134
overheating, 189–90

**P**

pack drive, 117–18
parasite control, 40–41
Paws Up command, 170–71, 208,
  209, 210, 221

performance-type visits
  handling multiple dogs, 200
  one-dog visits, 68
  personal interactions, changing
    to, 70–71
pet therapy, 4
petting
  accepting from strangers, 140–43
  class practice, 221
  therapeutic benefits of touch, 14,
    115
  as training motivator, 81–82
pinch collars, 139
platforms, use of, 207, 208–9
play
  teaching the retrieve, 92–98
  and teasing, 104–5
  as training motivator, 82
  using games in training, 88–89
positions-in-place training, 176–77
positive-negative touch ratio, 111
positive touch, 84
praise, use of, 80–81
problem solving, as training
  opportunity, 110
prong collars, 139
protection of dogs, 47, 48, 148
  corrections by others, 109, 121
  from disoriented people, 198–99
  dog fights, 54
  handler responsibility in, 151,
    188–89, 203–4
  injury from retrieving games, 97–
    98
psychiatric facilities
  aggression toward dogs, 48
  class discussion of, 223
  identification tags in, 191
  precautions in, 215–16
public access rights, 4, 36
publicity, and media coverage, 38–
  39, 184
public relations, social skills of
  handler-dog team, 147–62
public safety
  and control work training, 148–
    50
  courtesy to others, 157–60
pulling, as walking skill, 175
puppies
  bite inhibition, teaching, 100–103
  evaluating, 26–28
  socialization, 82, 150

## R

"reading" people
  interpreting body language, 155–56, 202–3
  public courtesy, 157–60
recall training, 123–27
Red Cross, disaster work
  credentials, 50
registration identification, 57, 191, 201
registry organizations. *See* national registry organizations
rejection, dealing with, 71–73
  class practice, 221
Release commands, 91, 94, 96, 130–31
reliability, testing the training, 124, 149
repetition, use of in training, 109, 154
resident animals, 48–49, 61, 196
retirement
  arthritis in dogs, 209–10
  hand signals as vision check, 167
  veterinarian assessment, 43
retrieving, 92–98
  games, safety precautions for, 97–98
  hand signal, 168–69
reward-correction ratio, 111
role-playing, class practice, 220–21
room-to-room visits, 68–70

## S

safety precautions
  class practice, 221
  for retrieving games, 97–98
  on visits, 195–200
  *See also* protection of dogs
scents, and sniffing, 107, 211, 213
schools, and dog education
  programs, 49
screening tests
  for classes, 219
  dog aggression, 54–55
  stillness, and Stay command, 84–85
  temperament issues, 25, 55, 143, 149
seal it with a kiss technique, 103, 104

send away exercises, hand signals, 168–69
service dogs. *See* assistance dogs
session length (visits)
  group visits, 67–68
  handler input on, 192–93
  one-dog visits, 63, 67–68
Shake Hands command, 173–74
shyness (in dogs), 143
Side command, 175–76
Sit command, 127–29
  hand signals, 164–65
Sit-Stay command, 127–32, 220
slip collars, 138–39
smiles, value of, 159–60
snap-around collars, nylon, 138–39
sniffing, 107, 211, 213
socialization, 82
  of children to dogs, 15–16, 36–37
  as foundation for social skills, 147
social skills
  developing, 147–62
  of dogs, 36–37
  public courtesy, 157–60
  and public relations, 162
  training in public, principles for, 162
spaying, and therapy work, 25–26, 43
staff involvement
  aggression toward dogs, controlling, 48, 198–99, 203
  in arranging visits, 57–58
  personality conflicts, 58–59
  and resident complaints, 216
  support on visits, 65–66, 68–69
stairs, exposure to, 39
standards of service, 55–56, 63
Stand command, 140–43, 220
stand for veterinary examination, 42
statement of responsibility, 218
Stay command, 129–32
  class practice, 220
  in teaching stillness, 83–85
  Wait command, 175
stillness, and Stay command, 83–85
stress
  and disaster work, 51
  to dog, 73, 193–94
  effect on handler, 48, 53, 187
  interpreting dog's signs of, 197

and overwork, 193–94
swing Finish, 177–80, 197

**T**

tails, handler awareness of, 89–90
Take It command, 93–96
  hand signals, 168–69
teasing, 104–5
temperament
  evaluation of, 25, 55, 143
  and public safety, 149
temperament testing, 26–28, 233
territorial ranges
  fearful people and, 202–3
  handler attention to dog, 203–4
  handler understanding of, 202–11
therapeutic benefits, 7–22
  anticipation by residents, 20
  to children, 15–16
  depression, overcoming, 9
  to dog, 30–31
  to handler, 31–33
  the need to be needed, 17–18
  reality, orientation to, 7–8
  retrieving games, physical skills and, 19, 97
  social stimulation, 10–14
  of touch, petting and, 14, 115
therapeutic interactions. *See* visits, aspects of; visits, scheduling of
therapists, working with, 16–17, 19
therapy dogs
  comfort level of on visits, 68–70
  definition of, 3–4
  as housedogs, 39–40
  older dogs, care for, 209–10
  unsuitable candidates, 27–28, 149
  *See also* dogs, choosing a partner
therapy sessions, types of, 60, 70–71
therapy work
  competition conflicts, contrast in training techniques, 90–92, 117–18, 123, 137
  emotional stress on handler, 48, 53, 187
  handler commitment issues, 33–35, 182–83
touch, conditioning dogs to, 79, 80
  and bite inhibition, 100–103
  cuddling sessions, 112–15
  ears, handling of, 92

feet, handling of, 173–74
  mouth, handling of, 95
  petting as training motivator, 81–82
  positive-negative touch ratio, 111
  positive touch, 84
  tails, handling of, 89–90
toys, 91, 97, 245–46
trading, retrieved objects, 93
training: issues concerning
  benefits of, 146
  commands, following through on, 126
  competition obedience vs. therapy work, 33–35, 92, 117–18, 123, 137
  correction-reward ratio, 111
  corrections, careful use of, 108–11
  games, benefits of, 88–89
  goals for, 119–20
  information resources, 120
  instructor's philosophy and, 119–21
  intelligent disobedience, 121–22
  motivators, 79–82
  new experiences, exposure to, 39, 105–8, 209, 220
  positive touch, use of, 84
  praise, use of, 80–81
  problem solving, encouraging, 110
  public safety and, 148–50, 157–60, 163
  seal it with a kiss technique, 103, 104
  session length, 123
  testing reliability, 124, 149
  tone of voice, "dynamics" of, 125, 134, 181–82
  trainability, 29
  training in public, principles for, 162
  undesirable behaviors, redirecting, 103, 212
  *See also* commands; control work
treats
  giving safely, 171–73
  as lure in greeting, 144
  as motivation in training, 79, 90–91, 135, 140
  use of at veterinary clinic, 42
  on visits, 198
tricks, 183–84

Tucker, Michael, around-behind
Finish, 179–80
tug-of-war, 98–99

# U

uncontrolled animals, 53–55, 64–65
unregistered dogs, statement of
responsibility, 218

# V

vaccination certificates, 57, 199,
201
veterinarian, relationship with, 41–
44
visitation options, 47–50, 192–93
visits, aspects of
approaching people, 71–73
becoming comfortable on, 53, 75
cleaning up after dogs, 212
disease transmission, 200–201
dog as distraction, 206–7
games, safety precautions for,
97–98, 98–99
goals of, 60, 70–71
and grooming, 114–15
handler as interpreter, 211–13
handler-dog routine, changes in,
70–71
handler preparation, 186–87
mobility equipment, working
around, 72, 209, 220, 221
placement of dog, 205–6
session location, choosing, 59,
68–70
sessions, types of, 60, 70–71
staff support on, 68–69
temperature conditions, 189–90
treats, 171–73
when to say no, 187–89
visits, scheduling of, 192–93
and anticipation by residents, 20
frequency, and handler burnout,
20, 217
and heat cycles, 25
one-dog visits, 66
staff involvement in, 57–58
standards of service, 55–56, 63
Volhard, Jack and Wendy
drives, theory of, 117–18
training techniques, 95, 132
volunteering, 217
care facilities, choosing, 75–76

insurance issues, 24, 56, 199–200
without a dog, 37–38, 44–45, 56

# W

Wait command, 175
walkers, working around, 209, 220,
221
walking skills, 175–76
warm-up exercises, 210–11
water, provision for, 189–90
wheelchairs, 72, 220, 221
Front position, 177
Go Through command, 176

# Z

zoonotic diseases, 200–201